THAT INCREDIBLE BOOK, THE BIBLE
VOLUME I

THE BIBLE COMES ALIVE

A PICTORIAL JOURNEY
THROUGH THE
BOOK OF BOOKS

THAT INCREDIBLE BOOK, THE BIBLE
VOLUME I

THE BIBLE COMES ALIVE

A PICTORIAL JOURNEY THROUGH THE BOOK OF BOOKS

Dr. Clifford Wilson
with Barbara Wilson

New Leaf Press

First printing: April 1997

ISBN: 0-89221-349-3
Library of Congress Number: 97-65171

Cover design: Left Coast Design, Inc., Portland, OR

Acknowledgments

Many colleagues and friends have contributed to the writing of this series of books. Dr. Henry Morris has generously made a number of his own writings available, and he has also made valuable suggestions at various points: some paragraphs come directly from him. That has been especially true in relation to the early chapters of Genesis. His friendship and scholarly advice have been greatly appreciated.

Mr. Garry Stone is the education officer and staff lecturer at the Australian Institute of Archaeology. Years ago I was his supervisor for his master's degree, and it has been gratifying to see his academic progress. His professional "looking over my shoulder" has been a very real help. He has acted as archaeological consultant to this series. Garry has also been more than helpful in the production of many of the photographs.

Probably over half of the photographs were taken by me, but often only as slides. Garry has carefully re-photographed these and slides of his own, with professionally pleasing results. He has likewise reproduced other prints from the collection of the Australian Institute of Archaeology (with permission). A large number of these were brought together by myself in my years as director of that institute.

A small number of the photographs have come from other friends, including Clem Clack, Carl Baugh, Jean Gordon, Eddie Hagler, John Rogers, Andrew Snelling, and Barbara Baddeley Wilson. A few others have contributed their pictures over the years, and we sincerely thank them all. The original paintings by Mrs. Lisa Flentge were first produced for display at Bible Times Center in Missouri (our Creation and Biblical Archaeology Center). We are very grateful for her willing co-operation.

A very real vote of thanks goes to my sister Mrs. Ethel Collins. This project started out as a one-volume offering, but has grown to several. She has willingly accepted the changes, even though these have meant a very great increase in what has been required of her in typing the manuscripts. She has demonstrated patience, diligence, and efficiency in ways that have been quite remarkable. By my own observation I know that at times she has worked about 16 hours a day over several days. This has been "Ethel's project," and I thank her in the name of our Lord Jesus Christ.

Mrs. Kath Salomons, my secretary in Australia, brought the work together from Ethel's disks, and the final layout is largely her work.

My wife, Barbara, has been a tower of strength. She is a very special person — thank you, Barbara!

To all these (and others unnamed) I offer thanks in Jesus' name.

Clifford Wilson

Contents

> In this section we consider evidence for the historicity of the early chapters of
> Genesis. We include creation, the flood, long-living men, the Tower of Babel, and the
> Table of Nations. We recognize that literal history starts at Genesis 1, with records that
> must be taken as fact and not mere legend or folklore. Genesis and all of Scripture are
> inspired by the Holy Spirit of God.

> Abraham's City of Ur was magnificent, with beautiful golden vessels and jewelry.
> However, the city was blighted by its religious practices, some of which were abominable
> to God. With his father and other family members, Abraham moved out of Ur to the sister
> city of Haran. We examine visual evidence about the city of Beersheba, the destruction of
> Sodom and Gomorrah, and the tomb where Abraham and other patriarchs were buried. We
> touch on Rachel stealing her father's clay gods.

> We consider the promotion of Joseph, from prison to palace. We see a great deal of
> Egyptian background, including the correct use of Egyptian titles — both for Joseph and
> other officials. We finish on a sad note: "In a coffin in Egypt," but point on to the hope of
> Christ's resurrection, ascension, and return.

> In this volume of "The Bible Comes Alive" we consistently demonstrate the verac-
> ity of these Scriptures as remarkable history — and as the setting for authentic prophecies.

Foreword

Clifford Wilson is a man of the modern Christian Renaissance in the best sense of the word — archaeologist, theologian, linguist, psychologist, educator, writer, lecturer, world traveler. Even more importantly, he is a keen witness to the truth and power of biblical Christianity, witnessing with unusual effectiveness, both with a consistent Christian life and through a prodigious output of scholarly works of Christian evidences and exposition.

This new volume — the first in a series covering the entire Bible — may well be the most significant of all his many books. It is almost unique in its twofold appeal. First, it is a book of great value as a contribution to Christian apologetics, documenting pictorially the historical trustworthiness of the Bible in copious detail. Second, it is a work of beauty, profusely iillustrating the lands and events of the Bible more completely and incisively than anything ever published before, so far as I know.

I believe it will find an honored place in the most-used portion of the reference library of all those pastors and Bible teachers who believe and teach the Word of God in its full truth and life-changing power. But it will also be a book that everyday Christians will want to keep on their coffee tables, delightful to browse in, and edifying to read wherever it is opened.

I consider it a privilege to recommend the book, heartily and without reservation, to everyone. I first heard Dr. Wilson some 20 years ago, speaking on his weekly radio program, and always ending his message with a ringing declaration of the absolute truth of the Bible: "Thy Word is truth!" Since then, we have often met together, worked together, prayed together. He has graciously provided a number of exhibits in our ICR Museum of Creation and Earth History. In many ways, he has been both an esteemed colleague and a warm friend — tireless scholar and beloved Christian brother.

Consequently, I am glad to help introduce both Dr. Wilson and this outstanding book to what I trust will be the widest and most responsive audience he has ever served. You, my reading friend, have a delightful learning experience in store!

Henry M Morris
President Emeritus
Institute for Creation Research

A Brief Survey Of
"THE BIBLE COMES ALIVE"

The Bible is the world's most accurate history book, and that history starts from Genesis 1. The record of creation is factual, and not merely part of a legend such as the Babylonian creation epic known as *Enuma Elish* (after its first two words, "When above" — "When above the heavens had not been named. . . .") The flood of Noah's time actually happened, and men DID live for vast periods of time. There really were giants on the earth. "The Table of Nations" as recorded in Genesis 10 is "astonishingly accurate" (Professor W.F. Albright), including the details about Nimrod who established cities in Babylonia and Assyria. The record of the settlement on the Plain of Shinar, as given in Genesis 11, is now recognized as being a brief description of the early Sumerian civilization. In that same chapter we have the record of the building of the Tower of Babel and the confounding of the languages of mankind. A corrupted version has been found at Abraham's ancient city of Ur, and scholars have necessarily recognized that the Genesis record in the Bible is actual history.

Abraham and the other patriarchs were actual men who lived against historical backgrounds, and Moses did compile the records we now know as the Pentateuch, the first five books of the Bible. Jericho DID fall to Joshua's men as described in the Book of Joshua, and Saul's body and armor were placed in two temples on Beth-shean, despite earlier critical arguments that the record was wrong.

The critics also said that the Psalms of David should be dated 800 years after his time — to the Maccabean period. Professor W.F. Albright wrote that this argument was "absurd," as demonstrated by findings at ancient Ugarit in Syria. They showed that David used some Canaanite words in the Psalms. The background was Davidic, and not Maccabean.

Solomon had architectural blueprints for the construction of some of his buildings. He was an outstanding administrator, but he also made serious blunders. Soon after his death his kingdom was divided, and then the Assyrians came to greater prominence. Their "reign of terror," together with some of their contacts with the people of the Bible, are well-documented in recovered Assyrian records. After 70 years of captivity (as prophesied) the Israelites returned from Babylon, and the Cyrus Cylinder shows the background to this from the point of view of the Babylonians.

The Dead Sea Scrolls gave to the world Hebrew fragments of every book of the Old Testament except Esther — about 1,000 years earlier than previously known Old Testament documents in Hebrew. The Dead Sea Scrolls also pointed to a coming Messiah — who is so clearly presented in the New Testament Gospels. Some of the Dead Sea Scrolls community looked for FOUR Messiahs — but they all come together beautifully in the person of Jesus the Christ.

Recovered documents in the Fayum region of Egypt have demonstrated the integrity of the gospel writings, while other findings in Asia Minor have shown the fallacy of higher critical challenges to the integrity of Luke the Historian who wrote both the Gospel of Luke and the Acts of the Apostles. Egyptian and other findings have also thrown a great deal of light on New Testament words. Secular and religious writings alike have clearly demonstrated the way Koine Greek (the everyday language of the people) was correctly used by the New Testament writers.

These are some of the evidences considered in the several volumes of *The Bible Comes Alive*. In this first volume we go through the records of Genesis to the death of Joseph. We continually see the integrity of the Bible, God's Word of truth.

An Overview of Volume 1, Genesis

In Genesis 1 through 11 we see the superiority of the Bible records in such areas as creation, the flood, long-living men, the Tower of Babel, and the Table of Nations.

We proceed to the time of the Patriarchs, and examine the records about Abraham's city of Ur and her sister city of Haran — both worshipers of the moon god Nannar. We watch Abraham moving around the land of Canaan, living in tents with his family, never owning any land except the cave in which he buried Sarah.

We see the destruction of Sodom and Gomorrah, and we climb Mt. Moriah to watch as the Angel of the Lord holds back Abraham's hand when he was about to slay his son Isaac.

Family Disharmony

We wonder at the way Jacob would deceive his father, Isaac, and have some sympathy for Jacob's mother, Rebekah, as Jacob quickly moves away so as to avoid the wrath of his brother Esau, whose birthright he had taken.

We watch Jacob's sons as they sell their brother Joseph into Egypt, and we are gratified to see how Joseph eventually makes good, becoming second-in-command to the Pharaoh.

We are saddened to see the note on which the book ends, with Joseph dead and "in a coffin in Egypt." It is a tragic ending and a stark contrast to the magnificent commencement, "In the beginning, God created. . . ."

So we turn to Genesis, the book of beginnings, and we find much that is new and important to our faith.

SECTION I:

EARLY GENESIS IS FACTUAL HISTORY

Creation and Flood Tablets

Throughout this series we present evidence as to the constant integrity of Scripture. That integrity is demonstrated right from the early Genesis records, and it continues through to the Book of Revelation at the end of the New Testament.

These four tablets are a specific reminder of the superiority and originality of the Bible records. The Babylonian creation tablets *Enuma Elish* have grotesque absurdities, with gods cutting each other in half, making heaven out of one half and the earth from the other. Even the Ebla tablets, which are superior to the Babylonian tablets and attribute creation to one Great Being, still have a host of other gods waiting in the background, as it were.

The eleventh tablet of the Epic of Gilgamesh tells the story of the flood, and again it is dramatically inferior to the Bible record. The Bible has no saga of gods crouching in fear because they are frightened that the flood they had brought on the earth would wash them out of the vault of heaven. Nor do they come like flies to the sacrifice when it is offered by the flood survivor because they have been hungry while the flood was sweeping over the earth, with men not there to feed them.

In Section I we consistently see ways in which the divinely revealed Genesis records are superior to other records of early people.

Records about Creation and the Flood

Bible history starts at Genesis 1, and the early chapters of Genesis are records of factual history. Other peoples had distorted records such as these about creation and the flood.

Babylonian Tablets of Creation and the Flood

The Babylonian tablets of creation are known as *Enuma Elish* because of the first words of this epic, "When above. . . ." There are seven tablets, and they were found in Nineveh in the library of the Assyrian King Ashur-Bani-Pal who died in 625 B.C. (One is at the top center.) Scholars therefore claimed that the Bible record of creation in Genesis 1 could not have been written until the time of Ezra, about 500 years before Christ. However, other copies of *Enuma Elish* in fragmentary form have now been found, dating as early as the 18th century B.C.

In the 1970s news of yet another record of creation was announced, this time from the ancient city of Ebla, the modern Tell

Mardikh. This tablet (center left) pre-dated the Babylonian record by many centuries. It showed that creation, attributed to one great being, was known long before Moses' time.

The other two tablets (center right and bottom — elaborated later) are parts of ancient Babylonian records of the flood, greatly corrupted from the account given in Genesis.

Enuma Elish Again

Enuma Elish was grotesquely polytheistic, with relatively unimportant similarities to the Bible story, but far greater differences. The Bible record is dramatically superior, with God transcending creation. Man was created to be the friend of God and not merely His menial servant. There is nothing grotesque in the biblical record: it can be believed at every point, provided one is prepared to accept the fact of the eternal God.

The Babylonian Epic *Enuma Elish*

This tablet is named from the first words, "When above. . . ." The Bible record is the accurate one!

The position is very different with creation records outside the Bible. All other creation accounts begin with the space/time/matter universe already pre-existing. Then they attempt to speculate how it might have "evolved" into its present form.

Dr. Henry Morris comments that modern evolutionism begins as a "quantum fluctuation in a primeval state of nothingness."[1] This yielded an infinitesimal point of space/time, which inflated very rapidly in a "cold big whoosh," followed by the "hot big bang," with the infinitesimal universe thenceforth expanding to its present space/mass/time complex. Energy was transformed into various types of infinitesimal particles, with these elementary particles of matter developing through natural forces into complex systems. Pagan pantheism begins with elementary matter in various forms being developed into complex systems by gods and goddesses who personify various natural forces. Appropriately, Genesis records the direct creation of space ("the heaven"), of time ("in the beginning"), and of matter ("the earth") — the tri-universe, the space/time/matter continuum which constitutes our physical cosmos, in essentially its present form.

A God Cutting a Goddess in Two

This is a modern version of part of the epic Enuma Elish. *After a great contest, the god Marduk cut the crocodile goddess Tiamat in two, making heaven from one half, and earth from the other.*

Marduk Cuts Tiamat in Two
(A modern version of the god Marduk
cutting the crocodile goddess Tiamat in two.)

Genesis 1:1 states, "In the beginning God created the heaven and the earth."

The verse states that the Godhead is plural, for that ending "im" is the Hebrew masculine plural. The verb used ("bara" — created) is singular, and so we are told that "the Godhead, He created." Many scholars believe that thus we have implicit in the Old Testament the doctrine of the Trinity which becomes explicit in the New Testament.

Notice also that no attempt is made in that first verse of the Bible to prove the existence of God: the verse was recorded in the beginning of human history when no one doubted the fact of God. The Bible's approach is that of Psalm 53:1, "The fool has said in his heart, there is no God." It does not set out to philosophize, or to prove the existence of God almost as though He were a mathematical formula. He is, in fact, our personal and loving Heavenly Father.

How different all this is from *Enuma Elish* where the god Marduk cuts the crocodile goddess Tiamat in two, making the heavens from one half and the earth from the other!

Reed Dwellers at the River Euphrates

According to Enuma Elish, *the Rivers Euphrates and Tigris flowed through Tiamat's eyes.*

The River Euphrates as it Is Today

At Genesis 2:10-14 we read,

> And a river went out of Eden to water the garden; from thence it was parted, and became into four heads. The name of the first is Pison; that is it which compasses the whole land of Havilah, where there is gold; and the gold of that land is good: there is bdellium and the onyx stone. And the name of the second river is Gihon: the same is it that compasses the whole land of Ethiopia. And the name of the third river is Hiddekel: that is it which goes toward the east of Assyria. And the fourth river is Euphrates.

We discuss this further in our comments on the biblical flood. For the moment we notice that this Genesis passage clearly establishes the literal nature of the Garden of Eden: it was an actual place, and not just part of a fairy tale from the ancient past. How different this is from the Babylonian *Enuma Elish*! Not only did Marduk cut Tiamat in half for the creation of the heaven and the earth, but he caused the River Euphrates to flow through one of her eyes and the River Tigris through the other. . . . Nonsense!

Creation Tablet at Ebla

One of the most important finds at Ebla was a creation tablet ascribing the great works of creation to one great being, "Lugal." It was earlier than the Babylonian creation epic.

Creation Tablet Found at Ebla

It was of special interest to Bible students to hear that Professor Pettinato had announced the finding of a creation tablet that was in some respects similar to Genesis 1. By the time this tablet was written, the people of Ebla were worshiping hundreds of gods, yet the creation tablet itself was associated with "Lugal" — a word that literally meant "the Great One," and eventually came to mean "king."

When Professor Pettinato made this public (I was present, the location being Ann Arbor, Michigan), he stated that in this case Lugal, the Great One, was a reference to God — the great God who created the heavens, the earth, the sun, and the moon by His Word. (At that time the rest of the tablet had not been translated.) Later, Professor Pettinato's interpretation was somewhat modified, but he still referred to this one great God who created.

The implications for the documentary hypothesis were far-reaching — creation was known to man even before the times of Moses, with the early records of Genesis being written on clay tablets and handed down from father to son, until eventually they came into the hands of Moses. Presumably Abraham took them across the Fertile Crescent, even as happened with one of the early versions of the flood which was found at Megiddo, dating to about the time of the conquest of Canaan by the Hebrews.

The liberal idea that these records were first put into writing hundreds of years after the time of Solomon simply is fallacious. The Bible's own claims about early writings should be taken at face value, and the archaeological evidence endorses that. In fact, *if it were not for the spiritual implications,* there should be no question about believing in these records as coming from the times of man's earliest history. They involved eye-witness, factual recording, but they also involved divine inspiration: they were and are part of the inspired Word of God.

Babylonian Tablet with Colophon

In many ways there are dramatic differences between the records of Genesis and those of surrounding nations. Pictured at right is a colophon — a connecting link between clay tablets. This tells us that this was one of a series of such tablets.

When we come to the Genesis records we find that there are a whole series of such colophons, with the distinguishing words: "These are the generations of. . . ." This appears on each of the tablets so designated, being a brief history relating to a particular leader. This is basically telling us that the Genesis records were written on clay tablets, dating back to the times of the person so

Babylonian Tablet with Colophon

This colophon indicates that this is a continuation of a series of tablets, as also in Genesis.

named. It is interesting to find that the tablets seem to end at the time of the death of the leading figure whose tablet has just been presented. It is almost as though these precious documents are handed over at the time of the funeral service! Probably some of the narrative passages were first told by the person named, and soon put into writing by a close descendant.

Starting from creation, the Bible tablets are there in writing. This is, of course, dramatically different from the grotesque records of people such as the Babylonians. In the Bible we do not have absurd statements such as gods cutting each other in half, or man being made from the blood of an evil god mixed with clay.

The dignity and total acceptability of the Genesis record of creation is dramatically different from those other records which have become corrupted and distorted over the centuries.

Beehive Huts at Ebla in Syria

These huts at Tell Mardikh are similar to huts found in ancient Sumeria (modern Iraq). They show a dramatic difference from the fame and prosperity of earlier times.

Beehive Huts at Ebla

These beehive huts are remarkably similar to other huts dating to beyond 2000 B.C. in ancient Sumeria, the biblical Shinar. Tell Mardikh, the site of ancient Ebla, is on the main road between Damascus and Aleppo.

Professor Paolo Matthiae of Rome University has been excavating there since 1964, but his work was not spectacular until 1968 when his team produced a statue dedicated to the goddess Eshtar, and also bearing the name of Ibbit-Lim, a king of Ebla. This endorsed the positive identification of the city — it had previously been known in Sumerian, Akkadian, and Egyptian texts. Many thousands of tablets have now been recovered from this ancient Canaanite site.

One of the interesting facts is that some of the important structures at this site were only just beneath the surface. Yet nomads, local inhabitants, and (in more recent times) travelers from around the world have passed the site for centuries with scarcely a second look.

Excavators at Ebla

Italian Professors Paolo Matthiae (right) and Giovani Pettinato (left).

Professors Pettinato and Matthiae

On the left is Professor Giovani Pettinato and on the right is Professor Paolo Matthiae, scholars from the University of Rome. Professor Matthiae was the excavator who discovered the remarkable finds at Ebla and Professor Pettinato, called in from Rome by his compatriot Professor Matthiae, was the first epigrapher who was able to break the code of this ancient script at Ebla.

In lectures in the United States, when the findings were publicized, Professor Matthiae emphasized archaeological evidence such as the style of buildings and artifacts, whereas linguistics professor Pettinato majored on the newly-translated tablets. He especially emphasized biblical relationships. Well-publicized protests from some Syrian officials followed: They did not want a common background with Israel or biblical associations to be elaborated.

For various reasons there was a separation of the two leaders: Pettinato was soon no longer a member

Uncovering Written Records at Ebla

The findings at Ebla were important as to culture, with excellent examples of artifacts and structures, some dating to before 4,000 years ago. Some were close to the modern ground level.

of the Ebla team. In addition, despite rumors of thousands more tablets being recovered, at least a partial blanket of silence seems to have fallen over the recoveries at this site. The biblical world has been forced to wait with patience for what could be very exciting evidence for Old Testament backgrounds.

Where the Ebla Tablets Were Found

There was great excitement when some thousands of clay fragments were found at this site, and soon Professors Matthiae and Pettinato were able to give to the world startling new information about another civilization ready to lay claim to the title, "Cradle of Civilization." Quite quickly Professor Pettinato was even able to present the forgotten language of these ancient Paleo-Canaanite people.

This is where many of the tablets were found. There were literary texts with mythological backgrounds, incantations, collections of proverbs, and hymns to various deities. Rituals associated with the gods are referred to, many of those gods being known in Babylonian literature of the later period. Most of the tablets deal with economic matters, tariffs, receipts, and other commercial dealings. Various offerings to the gods were also elaborated upon.

There were also syllabaries of grammatical texts, making it possible to go from one language to another. One recovered vocabulary text contained nearly 1,000 translated words, and there were 18 duplicate copies.

Where the Tablets Were Found

Dr. Bryant Wood is pictured at Ebla. Large numbers of fragments were found in this room. Ebla had been known from other writings, but now its identity was clearly established. Ebla rivaled Sumeria and Egypt as "a cradle of civilization." Notice that buildings such as a temple and a palace were only inches below the covered mound.

This is a view of where the first massive cache of tablets was found — over 20,000 fragments (not "tablets" as was first announced, mainly because of a translation misinterpretation).

The total number of fragments found was four times more than the total of all the other similar age tablets found up to that time. It surely was the fulfillment of an archaeologist's dream.

We have seen that one interesting aspect of the finds at Ebla is that they demonstrate that this ancient Canaanite culture was virtually contemporary with other cultures in ancient Sumeria and Egypt. It is remarkable that each of the three claimants to the title of "cradle of civilization" (Sumerian, Egyptian, and Canaanite civilizations) goes back only some 5,000 years from the present time.

If man has been around for millions of years — or even one million years — it is strange that there is no real evidence of settled civilizations and culture as we think of them today, before 5,000 years ago. The Bible believer has no problem with this, for the record of Genesis is pointing to only thousands of years for early man.

Tablets from Ebla

Here are some of the tablets found at Ebla. We have said that a creation tablet was found among them. The fact that it attributed creation to one great being ("Lugal"), caused many scholars to recognize that records about creation were in written form 1,000 years before the time of Moses.

The Bible's recognition of early writings is very clear, and these Ebla tablets (ranging in size from about one inch to nearly two feet, and covering many subjects) again make it clear that writing was widespread in man's early history. Some of the Ebla tablets dated to about 2300 B.C.

At Genesis 5:1 we read, "This is the Book of the generations of Adam. In the day that God created man, in the likeness of God made He him." The use of the word "Book" in this connection strongly implies that reading and writing were utilized by man's earliest generations.

Tablets of Various Sizes

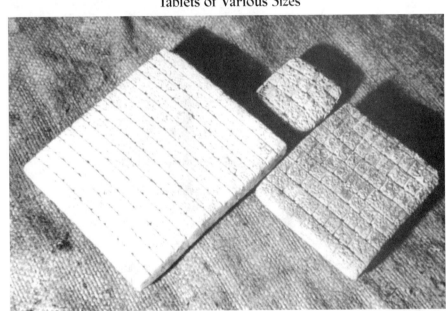

The tablets at Ebla were wide-ranging in size, from about one inch to nearly two feet. They dealt with many subjects such as trade, literature, dictionaries, and religious texts.

These Genesis records, finally edited and assembled by Moses, must originally have come from eyewitnesses. There is no reason why their transmission could not have been by written records instead of being orally repeated tales as higher critics had earlier claimed.

Economic Text at Ebla

*This particular text dated to about 2300 B.C. Others were several
hundred years nearer to our times. Trading tablets included the names
of a number of cities mentioned in the Bible.*

Economic Tablet from Ebla

This is one of the larger economic texts from Ebla, dating to about 2300 B.C. Professor Matthiae states (in *Ebla — An Empire Rediscovered*) "It is clear from the Archive texts that the distribution of the merchandise was totally organized by the State." The geographic area covered by trade was astounding — it "extended from the Mediterranean coast in the west to the Tigris valley in the east, and from Central Anatolia in the north to Palestine in the south. . . ." Mari, Assur, and Haran are among the important trade centers referred to. Even Damascus is known in the form DIMASHQI. Jerusalem, Megiddo, and Lachish are included among Israel contacts.

Ebla was trading in many commodities, including metallurgy, tools, weapons, ornaments, and furniture. In his section dealing with the economic life of Ebla, Professor Matthiae tells of "huge quantities of gold and silver" being "received in tribute or in payment for merchandise" (far exceeding Solomon's stated wealth!) "The economic structure . . . must certainly have been extremely complex and highly developed." All this was back about 2300 B.C. Clearly, "the position of Ebla must have been of extraordinary vitality and fundamental importance. . . . Its contribution to the diffusion of urban civilization in the Near East was undoubtedly exceptional and intensely original in form." [2]

Searching for a Place to Live

As small family groups separated from the others and migrated from Babel (Gen. 11:9), they must have searched for a place to settle down and establish their own homeland. Presumably the stronger and more intelligent clans laid claim to the nearest and most productive regions; others kept on traveling until they could find a suitable location that was not yet claimed by others. Some would even have to live in caves, and so the concept of "cavemen" would quickly develop.

This meant living by hunting animals and gathering wild fruits and vegetables for food, and using sticks and chipped stones such as those pictured here, for tools and weapons. It also often meant living in grass huts or caves for shelter.

Flint and Other Stone Axheads

Axheads are found in sites as separated as Sumeria and Australia. Some are called Paleolithic (Old Stone Age) and others Neolithic (New Stone Age), yet often they are indistinguishable.

Urbanization is usually considered to be one of the first indicators of the emergence of true civilization from the hunting and food-gathering stage (the so-called Stone Age culture). We read of the Paleolithic (Old Stone Age) and the Neolithic (New Stone Age) but arrowheads and other artifacts from Australia (Neolithic) and Sumer (Paleolithic), for example, are virtually indistinguishable. It is significant that true civilized cultures have existed since the very first generation following Adam, with no suggestion whatever of a long evolutionary advance from an imaginary Stone Age.

Pottery Mold for Casting Bronze Implements

Anthropologists have usually divided human pre-history into several divisions, supposedly marked by the evolutionary stage of culture that had been achieved. The Paleolithic Era is said to have begun when man had essentially completed his biological evolution and was just beginning his cultural evolution.

However, right through the supposedly different ages there has been overlap. This pottery mold, used for casting bronze implements, comes from Shechem in Israel. Man is unique in his ability to make one utensil in order to mass produce others.

Cross-cultural patterns and trading exchanges at Shechem and other Israelite cities mean that such

Mold for Casting Bronze Implements

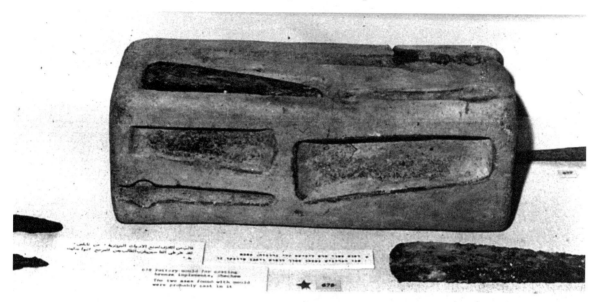

This pottery mold from Shechem was used for casting bronze implements.

terms as "Bronze Age" and "Iron Age" must be held only lightly. Geography, climate, availability of crops, strong leadership, and so much more meant dramatic differences — with so-called late developments in early areas, and vice versa.

Intelligence, technology, and cultural advance are not related to man's reaching any particular evolutionary stage. These facts oppose the widely taught theories of many modern scholars.

Metallurgy in Ancient Civilizations

Weapons like these bronze spearheads and axeheads have been found right through the ages. The idea of a strict Bronze Age demanding a particular time period should not be insisted on. Bible clues are relevant.

In Genesis 4 we read of early men who could handle the harp and the organ, while Tubal-Cain was an instructor of every craftsman in brass and iron. It is not so long since this also was seriously challenged, it being argued, for instance, that iron was not known so early. However, one example of iron being used well before the time of Abraham is with the chariot rings of the famous Queen Pu-Abi who was buried in the royal death pits at Abraham's city of Ur. (We discuss these when we come to the time of Abraham.)

Meteoritic iron was used at various other places, and the biblical record is totally acceptable. In fact, the elements associated by evolutionary archaeologists with the emergence of civilization among civilized backgrounds are precisely those systems that were invented by the descendants of Cain — domestication of animals and metallurgy, as well as agriculture and city building that were first practiced by Cain himself.

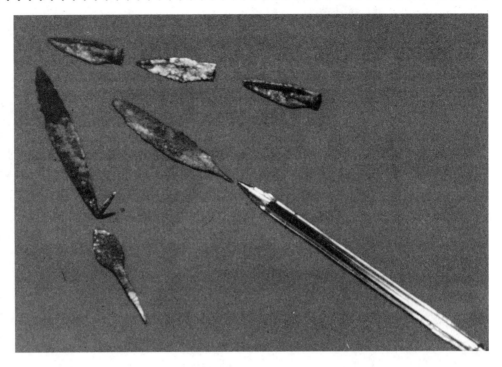

Bronze Javelin and Arrowheads

These bronze arrowheads and a javelin from Gaza date to the so-called Late Bronze Age. Similar weapons have been recovered from many sites, dating to very early times.

The Early Manufacture of Pottery and Metal

Early people knew how to work pottery and metal, including axeheads such as this one from Egypt. However, such knowledge was useless after the flood until they could find adequate sources of metals, clays, and building materials. Similarly, they knew how to raise crops and domesticate animals, but the establishment of such sources of food and clothing would take many years. Right from early times there was considerable interchange across the countries of the "Fertile Crescent."

Bronze Age Ax

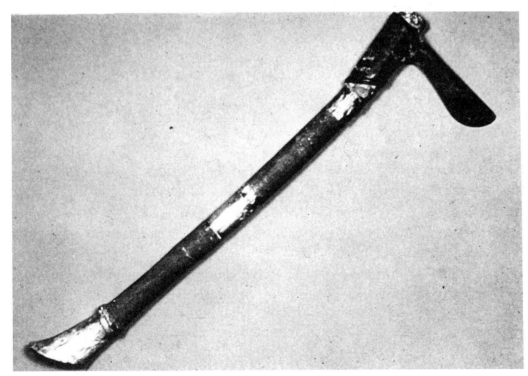

The production of Egyptian bronze axes required high intelligence and technological ability.

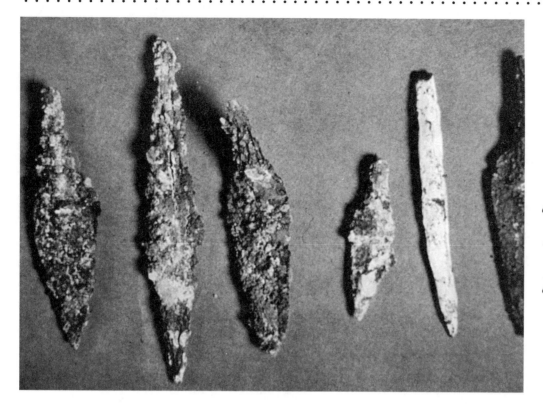

Bronze Weapons from Various Sites

These weapons are from Ancient Times House, the museum center of the Australian Institute of Archaeology. It houses implements and weapons from various ancient sites and times.

So it is that wherever one looks around the world at each site suitable for human cultural habitation, it seems that there is always evidence of a Stone Age culture when that site was first occupied. Later occupations (or later periods of the original occupation) indicate higher cultures. This was not because of slow evolutionary development, but because of such changes as rapid growth of populations, development of specializations, locations of sources of metals and building materials, and establishment of stable supplies of food and clothing. When a culture was interrupted (by an outside invasion, for example) the latter (if successful) had usually come from a center of still higher culture which had then transplanted to the new site.

Artifacts from Ancient Civilizations

These rusted weapons in the museum of the Australian Institute of Archaeology have been found at various ancient habitations, and they date to different time periods. They do not reflect man's slow cultural evolution, but rather they show the drama of post-diluvian, post-Babel man being forced by God to "be fruitful and multiply and fill the earth" (Gen. 9:1). That is what God had commanded in the first place.

The vast period of time assigned for the "Stone Age" by many modern scholars (from one to four million years and even more) is purely conjectural, based mainly on the arbitrary and unrealistic uniformitarian assumptions of the potassium-argon dating technique.

Even the dates assigned for the beginning of civilization (about 8000 B.C.) are based on similar unrealistic assumptions in the radio-carbon method. It is amazing that so many scientists and other scholars can blithely believe and teach that man's physical evolution was completed about one million years ago, but that he then stagnated in a cultural rut and began his cultural evolution only (so they say) about 10,000 years ago!

Neanderthal Man — and Where These Were Identified

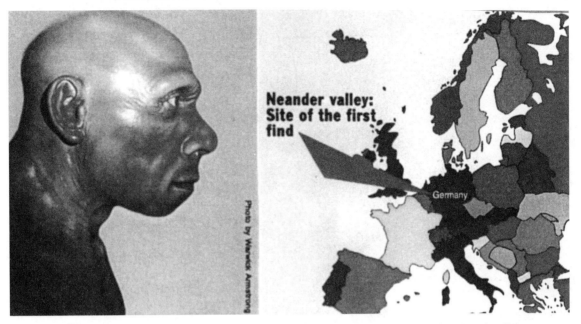

This reconstruction of "Neanderthal Man" and the relevant map is used by courtesy of the Creation Science Foundation, Brisbane, Australia.

Neanderthal Man

Neanderthal Man was fully human, so named because some of them were found in the Neander Valley in Germany. It appeared they endured food and vitamin deficiencies and had problems such as rickets.

It has always been possible for a tribe of a higher culture to deteriorate to a lower level for various reasons — immorality, disease, dwindling populations, etc. There are many "Stone Age" people living today (and all through history) in African and South American jungles, in New Guinea, and other places. Most of these tribes give evidence of having known a much higher level of culture in their distant past.

Olduvai Gorge in Tanzania

Dr. Louis Leakey and his wife, Mary, found the skull of Zinjanthropus Bosei (East-Africa Man) at the Olduvai Gorge, and it attracted worldwide attention. This excavation was sponsored by the National Geographic Society and it received wide publicity. Leakey claimed that it was the earliest pre-human skull ever recovered, being nearly two million years old. Later what appeared to be a man-made circular structure was found at an earlier level, and Leakey eventually admitted two things:

1. The skull was apparently no more than 10,000 years old; and

2. It was not human but was a variety of Australopithecus ("southern apes"). It is an unfortunate fact of life that a documentary indicating that this was a sensational find was still being presented over American television years after Dr. Leakey had died of a heart attack.

In *Time* magazine of April 24, 1964, page 68 we read,

Now Dr. Leakey has changed his mind. He now believes that Zinjanthropus was an Australopithecine, a non-human vegetarian of low intelligence and not a toolmaker.

Model of Olduvai Gorge, Tanzania

This is the Olduvai Gorge where Dr. Louis Leakey found Zinjanthropus — at first claimed to be a near-human nearly two million years old. Later evidence caused him to change his mind.

In *Evolution: The Fossils Still Say No!*, Dr. Duane Gish comments: "These animals (Australopithecus Bosei and Australopithecus Robustus — Ed.) thus, unquestionably had the brains of apes. . . ."[3] They were NOT transitional forms — or missing links as they were once called.

"Australopithecus Robustus"

"Skull 71" on the left is "Lucy," found by anthropologist Donald Johanson. On the right is "Skull 48," from Swartkrans in South Africa . . . not man and wife after all, but separate ape species. For many years anthropologists claimed that the various forms of Australopithecines were transitional forms between apes and humans. The first highly publicized example was the specimen recovered by Dr. Raymond Dart in 1924. Subsequent findings have caused many scholars to turn from

Australopithecines Were Not Humans

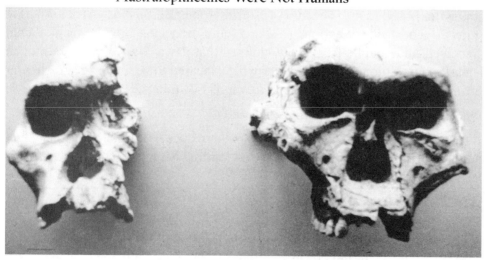

"Skull 71" on the left is "Lucy." "Skull 48" is on the right.

these creatures as ancestors to man: their brains are much smaller than those of humans, and their skulls, jaws, and ears are distinctively ape-like. Even their supposed bi-pedal upright walking is explained on the same basis that modern apes also often walk uprightly.

Lord Solly Zuckerman (famous British anatomist) and Dr. Charles Oxnard (Professor of Anatomy at the University of Southern California Medical School) have demonstrated by multivariate analysis the non-human physical make-up of the Australopithecines. They were as far removed from apes and humans as apes and humans were from each other. The conclusions from Lord Zuckerman's team follow 15 years of research. Oxnard wrote, "Although most studies emphasize the similarity of the Australopithecines to modern man . . . a series of multivariate statistical studies of various post-cranial fragments suggests other conclusions."[4]

There are also many modern examples of people being taken from so-called "Stone Age" cultures, being trained in Western technology and education, and becoming highly competent leaders in various disciplines. Humans are human, no matter what their culture. Humans don't become apes, and apes don't become humans.

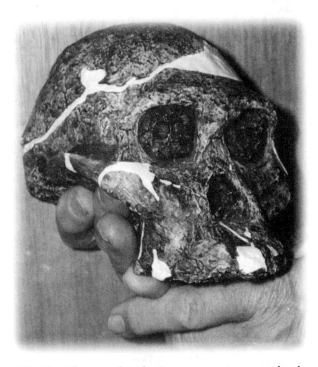

The Gracile Australopithecines were not supposed to be as strong as their Robustus relatives, but shared similar physical features. Both varieties are now recognized as apes, not humans.

Gracile Australopithecus

Gracile Australopithecus is not as heavily built as Australopithecus Robustus and at one time it was argued that they were female and male respectively. That argument has now largely been put aside, and it is recognized that they are the same species — not human but, as their name indicates, "southern apes."

They join many other "transitional forms" as not being that after all. Thus, Colorado Man's tooth proved to come from the horse family; Ramapithecus was an extinct ape; Kenyapithecus was a form of orangutan or gorilla; Nebraska Man (and his wife!) turned out to be a peccary, an extinct pig; Java Man was an ape after all.

The findings of Donald Johanson, such as "Lucy" — Australopithecines at Hadar in Africa — are likewise rejected as hominid. In *Ape-Men — Fact or Fallacy*, Dr. Malcolm Bowden says in a survey of Johanson's work: "It is my consideration that all the fossils discovered so far in Hadar are simply those of various apes, whose supposed human characteristics do not bear even superficial examination."[5]

Piltdown Man

When the "finding" of Piltdown Man by Charles Dawson was first announced in 1912 it was hailed as the greatly sought-after breakthrough. Here, it seemed, was the "missing link" between apes and men: at last Charles Darwin was vindicated and in the process the biblical story of the creation of man was finally put to rest.

Piltdown Man

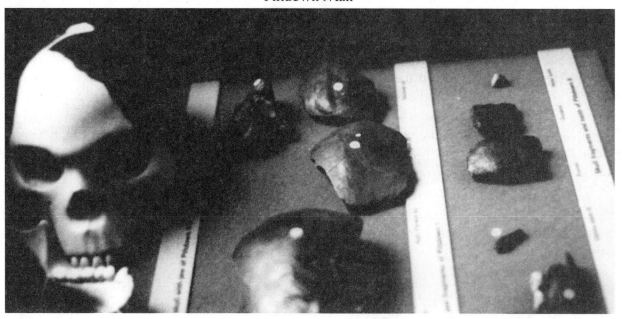

One of the most famous "missing links" was the extraordinarily successful hoax, Piltdown Man. The original fossils in the British Museum are shown on the right.

The fact is, of course, that eventually the scientific establishment exposed Piltdown Man as a fraud. It was so called because it supposedly came from a gravel pit at Piltdown in East Suffolk, England. For about 40 years it was accepted as a classic example of the evolution of man. (I was told by an Indonesian Pacific College Master's candidate in 1990 that it is still taught as fact in Indonesia.)

"Piltdown Man" was actually a faked skull, carefully constructed by making use of altered and stained bones from an orangutan and a modern man. The teeth were filed down. (During 1990 the perpetrator of the hoax was named as the late Sir Arthur Keith.)

A model of Piltdown Man is seen on the left of the above picture, with the separate bone fragments on the right.

Eugene Dubois

What about Java Man?

Eugene Dubois, a Dutch physician, went to Java in 1887 determined to find the "missing link." Java Man *(Pithecanthropus Erectus)* resulted. "Java Man" derived from a few teeth, a skull cap, and a leg bone found in Indonesia in 1891 and 1892. The leg bone was found 14 meters (45 feet) from the skull cap, but the two were linked together to make the "missing link." Dubois first found two human skulls at the same site, these being known as the Wadjak skulls, but he did not give information about these to the scientific world until 30 years later in 1920.

This caused considerable consternation, for though the leg bone he displayed was probably human, the skull was more ape-like. As two human skulls were also found at the same time, in similar dated strata, it could not be argued that the other skull was a transitional form between ape and man. Because Dubois had actually gone to Java to find the "missing link," his ape skull answered reasonably well when first put before the scientific community.

Dubois himself later admitted it was probably the skull of a giant gibbon.

Decline of Integrity

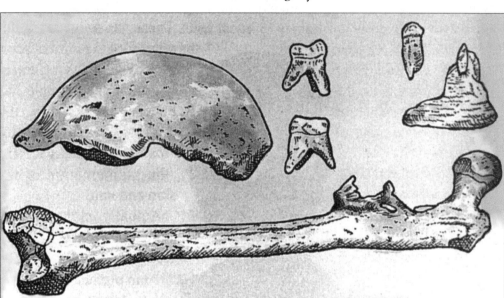

The leg bone looks like an ordinary human one, although the skull cap differs from the average human type. Because of the similarities to ordinary humans, Pithecanthropus erectus *("upright ape-man"), as paleontologists once knew him, is now* Homo erectus *("upright human").* Homo erectus *fossils have now been found in the same strata as average human type fossils, so they appear to be just a variant of the human kind, not an ancestor.*

A Decline in Scientific Integrity

The scientific integrity of Eugne Dubois has been seriously questioned. This is illustrated by a comment from Professor W.R. Thompson, F.R.S., in his Introduction to the Centenary edition of Darwin's *Origin of the Species:*

The success of Darwinism was accompanied by a decline in scientific integrity. . . . A striking example, which has only recently come to light, is the alteration of the Piltdown skull so that it could be used as evidence for the descent of man from apes; but even before this a similar instance of tinkering with evidence was finally revealed by the discoverer of Pithecanthropus, who admitted, many years after his sensational report, that he had found in the same deposition bones that are definitely human. Though these facts are now well-known, a work published in 1943 still accepts the diagnosis of Pithecanthropus given by Dubois, as a creature with a femur of human form permitting an erect posture.

Bangalore Man

This photograph was taken by me in Bangalore, southern India, in 1952. The man pictured was a well-known identity, and the schoolchildren in the area were able to tell quite a lot about his background. He was taken around by a man who was almost his "keeper," and, unfortunately, this poor deformed man was the butt of many jokes.

Bangalore Man was no missing link, no transitional form, but simply a poor fellow with a congenital deformity that had left him with virtually no brain capacity. Some children are born with no legs or no arms, and there are many known cases of children being born with virtually no brain. Such was the case with Bangalore Man — not a missing link between apes and men, but a person who was fully human but with a deficiency.

All the so-called transitional forms between apes and men are either fully apes or fully men. There is no such thing as a "missing link."

Bangalore Man Again

After a lecture I gave, one newspaper report stated that I had shown the twin brother of Neanderthal Man. Neander-

A Man with a Genetic Abnormality

Dr. Clifford Wilson photographed this man in Bangalore, India, in 1952. He was fully human despite his serious genetic abnormalities. He was no ape-man, but was born with devastating congenital deficiencies.

thal Man, from the Neander Valley in Germany was a true human, again with deficiencies. At the time it was clear that the reporter meant that Bangalore Man was a "missing link."

The once fashionable names of Java Man, Piltdown Man, Nebraska Man, Heidelberg Man, Rhodesia Man, Peking Man, and others used to be offered as proof of "missing links," pointers to man's evolution. They are nowadays all but ignored in anthropological discussions. Neanderthal Man and Cro-Magnon Man are universally accepted as Homo Sapiens today.

Bangalore Man was nowhere near as capable as a normal human. As some humans have been born without arms or legs, so this man was born with almost no brain capacity — but he was still human.

Not only have sensational "missing links" been put aside, but dates also have been dramatically reduced. One example is "Keilor Man," Keilor being a suburb on the outskirts of Melbourne, Australia.

When the skull was found there was the usual loud declaration about another "missing link," and the age of 150,000 years was given for this early man. Carbon dating came into its own, and soon a new age of 9,000 was tentatively accepted — and that is not necessarily final.

The Epic of Gilgamesh

This is The Epic of Gilgamesh, *found at Nineveh in the Assyrian palace of King Ashur-Bani-Pal who died about 625 B.C. In a crude form, it outlined the great flood.*

The Gilgamesh Epic

The Gilgamesh epic was written on 12 tablets, and — like the Babylonian creation epic *Enuma Elish* — it, too, was found in the library of the Assyrian King Ashur-Bani-Pal at Nineveh. The flood record was found on Tablet No. 11. As with the creation tablet, other fragments of this epic are now known, dating to many hundreds of years earlier than the copy from Ashur-Bani-Pal's palace, to even before the times of Moses. (Moses would have compiled the Genesis record from earlier divinely supervised tablets already in existence.)

There are similarities to the biblical flood record but, as with creation, there are much greater dissimilarities. The Bible record is superior and is historically acceptable. In fact, the history of *The Epic of Gilgamesh* is seriously distorted, and there are evidences of superstition and un-godlike behavior which are certainly not to be found in the Genesis record.

It is all very different from the majestic and totally acceptable record in Genesis. There is no superstition, no magic or grotesque absurdities in the biblical record. It is straightforward, factual history.

Fragment of *Gilgamesh Epic* Found at Megiddo

Another fragment of *The Epic of Gilgamesh* was found at the Israelite city of Megiddo. Megiddo is the New Testament "Armageddon," which literally means Mount Megiddo (Har Megiddo).

The fragment cannot be dated exactly because it was actually found in an archaeological rubbish dump. However, scholars date it to about 1400 B.C. — that is, approximately to the time of Moses.

Fragment of *Gilgamesh Epic* Found at Megiddo

This must have been carried about 1400 B.C. across the Fertile Crescent to Megiddo in Israel.

If this fragment of the Babylonian *Epic of Gilgamesh* could have been carried across the Fertile Crescent, it is a reminder also that Abraham could have carried the Genesis records with him when he traveled from Ur to Haran, and then eventually (after his father died) down into the Promised Land.

There is good reason to believe that eventually the clay tablets on which the Genesis records were written came into the hands of Moses and that he then edited and compiled them for inclusion in the Pentateuch, the first five books of the Bible.

Flood Tablet Fragment Found at Nippur

The area outlined in black in the photo below is a record about the flood. It was a different version from *The Epic of Gilgamesh*. The huge size of the vessel pointed to the story growing over time. It reminds us that there are many records of the flood. Over 300 are known around the world, with about 30 of them in writing. Some are remarkably close in their details to the story told in the Bible. It becomes clear that the original is, in fact, the Bible story.

Professor W.F. Albright concluded that "the Bible record contains archaic features dating it to before any Mesopotamian version that is preserved in cuneiform sources"[6] Such statements illustrate the authenticity of these early Genesis records. The Bible record is not just a purified version of the Babylonian epic. Rather, the Babylonian record is a distortion of the biblical original.

Flood Tablet from Nippur

This fragment came from Nippur, in the same general area that Abraham came from.

Professor Albright did not always have such a high view of the biblical record, and his honest reassessment is important as a recognition of some changed views toward the early Genesis records. He was renowned as a leading linguist in various cuneiform and other ancient scripts.

"The Gods Came Like Flies"

The grotesque Epic of Gilgamesh *talks of the gods cowering like dogs as the flood waters rose, then coming like flies to the sacrifice that Utnapishtim (the "Babylonian Noah") offered.*

"The Gods Came Like Flies"

In the Babylonian Epic of Gilgamesh we read that the gods were terrified as they saw the floodwaters rising higher and higher. The epic says that they "cowered like dogs." Then the Babylonian gods began to blame each other for having taken such drastic action, instead of just letting a few wild animals loose on men. We can hardly imagine such descriptions in the record given in Genesis!

When the floodwaters subsided the Babylonian Noah, Utnapishtim, came out from the ark and sacrificed a lamb to the gods. They had not been fed by men while the floodwaters were ascending, and we read that now they came like a swarm of flies to the sacrifice.

Gods in terror? Cowering like dogs? Hungry, having to be fed by men? How unbelievable! It is all so very inferior to the majestic story told in Genesis, a record that is totally acceptable, provided we accept the concept of God with His attributes of righteousness and justice.

Noah's Ark

A vessel such as this was necessary to withstand the tremendous forces let loose when "the fountains of the great deep were broken up." Its measurements were ideal.

Noah's Ark

Noah's ark has always intrigued Bible students. Noah was told to build a vessel 300 cubits long, 50 cubits wide, and 30 cubits high. In early times there were several different measurements for the cubit, with variations between the Babylonian, Egyptian, and Hebrew measures. In fact, the Hebrews themselves had two different measures — a long cubit of 20.4 inches (Ezek. 40:5) and a common cubit of about 17.5 inches (the measurements given on the famous Siloam tunnel inscription in Jerusalem verify this).

Noah might well have employed workmen, for this vessel was massive, with a gross tonnage of 14,000 tons or more — equal in size to some modern ocean liners.

Although there have been sensational and unsubstantiated claims about the ark, some sightings through the centuries appear to have been genuine. A monastery at the base of Mt. Ararat was a repository for many artifacts supposedly recovered from the ark. It was destroyed by an avalanche in 1840.

The record in Genesis 6 through 8 clearly indicates that the flood was worldwide and a vessel such as the ark was essential for the preservation of Noah, his family, and the representative animals. At that time "all the high hills under the whole heaven were covered" (Gen. 7:19).

Fossilized Trilobite

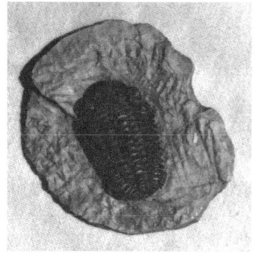

This trilobite was found in the Medusa Quarry of Silica in Ohio.

A Fossilized Trilobite

This is a trilobite, a three-lobed creature supposedly dating to over 300 million years ago when it (again, supposedly) became extinct. However, trilobites have turned up in various geological strata, even with man-made artifacts) quite out of their "index" dating period.

Many creatures did indeed die out as a result of the flood. During the centuries after the devastation of the flood, many of the great animals that had come off the ark (though they survived and proliferated for a time) eventually were unable to cope with the drastic changes in climate and environment, and they became extinct. The flood itself dramatically altered the face of the earth, and the atmosphere was affected by reduced oxygen pressure — meaning that animals and humans would not grow so big or live as long as previously.

There were other catastrophic effects also, such as the problems associated with the process of glaciation in the so-called "Ice Ages" — these being post-flood and not pre-flood. Then there were the awful devastations from active volcanoes and the very breakup of the continents as the original one tectonic plate on which the earth rested was broken up into several smaller plates. The effect on life-forms was very great.

Nevertheless there have been many examples of "extinct" creatures being found to still exist after all. The geological column should no longer be accepted as a standard for dating various life forms. Even carbon dating has demonstrated that vast numbers of fossils should be dated to about 5,000 years ago. Fossils are formerly live things that have been suddenly overwhelmed and encased, their forms thus being preserved. Almost all fossils are a consequence of the biblical flood.

Polystrate Coal Fossils

Dr. Andrew Snelling writes about this fossil formation:

The location is called Quarries Head just to the south of Caves Beach, Newcastle (New South Wales, Australia), and was first reported by Sir Edgeworth David, professor of geology at the University of Sydney in his 1907 report on "The Geology of the Hunter River Coal Measures, New South Wales," published as the *Geological Survey of New South Wales Memoir G4*. The photograph shows two tree stumps on top of the Lower Pilot Seam and at least one tree stump sticking up above the Upper Pilot Seam, silhouetted against the sky. When David reported on these tree stumps in his 1907 report many of them were true polystrate fossils, the tree stumps going all the way from the Lower Pilot Seam right up into the Upper Pilot Seam.

Polystrate Coal Fossils

Here we have fossilized trees extending through more than 20 feet of coal in the Newcastle area of New South Wales, Australia.

The tree stumps have their roots broken off, so they couldn't have grown where they are now fossilized, but had to be transported in and buried this way. Many of the tree stumps were still true polystrate fossils in 1964 when Beryl Nashar, then the professor of geology at the University of Newcastle, published her book, *The Geology of the Hunter Valley*. The tree stumps that are shown in this photograph are only a portion of those exposed that remain, the rest being removed by the forces of weathering and erosion, plus vandalism and sample-takers.[7]

A Tree Through Coal Seams

Around the world there are many examples of trees such as this one from that same area near Newcastle, encased by several strata of coal. At times they are even upside-down: they could not have grown there. They have been transported by water and rapidly encased by a series of coal seams within days — not millions of years or even centuries.

Polystrate Tree Fossil Near Newcastle, Australia

The fossilized tree in this photograph from near Swansea Heads, N.S.W., Australia, is black because the bark has been turned to coal. The tree sits on the Lower Pilot Seam, just beneath and behind the shovel. The Upper Pilot Seam is at the top of the photograph. The layering in the volcanic ash is quite evident. The picture on the previous page is from the same location.

Dr. Snelling further states that these fossilized trees have been interpreted by evolutionary geologists as representing the remains of the last forest to grow in the peat swamp that is now represented by the Lower Pilot coal seam, yet their roots have been broken off and they are pine trees of a type (Dadaxylon) that cannot grow healthily in peat swamps. One is forced to conclude that the trees did not grow here, but were catastrophically transported and deposited here, otherwise they would not have been preserved as fossils. Polystrate tree fossils point to one great catastrophe — the biblical flood. Polystrate fossilized trees are trees running through several strata, including various forms of rock. Sometimes the trees are upside-down. There is no satisfactory explanation for their location except that the trees were transported and then encased by the strata that (necessarily) rapidly succeeded each other.

Many coalfields have large numbers of coal-bearing strata, interbedded with rocks and other materials. The strata thickness varies from a few inches to several feet. The evidence is that massive amounts of plant and tree materials have been transported to each location. There are massive accumulations of such plants and trees. The evidence of polystrate fossils is convincing as to ONE great flood.

Gilgamesh and the Babylonian Story of the Flood

People had departed from the worship of the one true God. They made images of men, women, animals, and creeping things. Their hero, Gilgamesh, is third from the left — a deified man.

Gilgamesh and the Babylonian Story of the Flood

The third figure from the left is Gilgamesh, the legendary ruler of the ancient city-state of Uruk, and he was supposed to be two-thirds god and one-third man. The story of the flood is told on the 11th of the 12 tablets making up the epic.

Utnapishtim was the Babylonian Noah, and with his boatman Pussur-Amurri he went through seven days of terrible flood. Enkidu, the very good friend of Gilgamesh, had died at the decree of the gods and Gilgamesh realized that he, too, must eventually die. He hears of one who has escaped death and sets off to find him so that he can learn the secret of immortality. Alongside a great sea he meets Siduri the Ale-wife who provides the beer needed for travelers on the sea.

After crossing the sea, known as the "waters of death," he at last finds Utnapishtim, the only man who had ever found everlasting life. Utnapishtim speaks to Gilgamesh, and learns of his sadness at the death of his friend Enkidu, and of his sorrow as he wandered up and down pondering the great mystery of life and death. He asks Utnapishtim how he had come to stand in the assembly of the gods and find everlasting life. Utnapishtim tells the story of how one of the gods urged him to destroy his house and to build a vessel into which he was to bring representative living creatures.

The epic goes on to tell in detail how Utnapishtim built the great boat which needed 30,000 baskets of pitch, and the great flood came after he and his family were safely aboard.

Monastery on Mount Ararat

The Monastery of St. James on Mount Ararat was destroyed in June 1840

The Monastery of St. James on Mount Ararat

This picture of the Monastery of St. James on Mt. Ararat is enlarged from a drawing reproduced by Lisa Flentge. It was in the book *Journey to Ararat* by Dr. J.J.F. Parrot, published in 1845 (p. 164).

This is the monastery that housed artifacts recovered from the ark over many centuries. Artifacts are commonly associated with ancient civilizations or other recovered sites. They help us to understand patterns of life and cultural practices. Local people in the area of Mount Ararat have produced what they claim are artifacts from Noah's ark over many years, insisting that the ark itself has been entered many times when there have been constant long summers over long periods, meaning that at such times the ice line is higher and the ark is exposed.

Pictures of many of these artifacts were shown to this author in the late 1960s by highly reputable New Zealand archaeologist Hardwick Knight who had shown great interest in ark research for many years.

Long-Living Men

In Genesis 5 there are details of men who lived for hundreds of years. The effects of sin and disease were not as great then as they are now, and the climate was probably much more uniform before the flood. This is hinted at in the Sumerian king list (pictured) found at ancient Kish. That king list tells of kings who lived BEFORE THE FLOOD — they supposedly lived for thousands of years. Recent research has suggested that the Babylonian figures can be translated differently and that, in fact, the

This Sumerian king list was found at Kish, south of Baghdad. It tells of ten kings who lived for thousands of years each — BEFORE THE FLOOD. After the flood life spans were more "normal."

Long-Living Men

ages might have been very similar to those in Genesis. This involves a system based on decimals rather than one based on sixties.

The excavators at Kish also found evidence that in the early days of the city's history the occupants thought in terms only of a sky god, an earth god, and a sun god. They further believed that the original god was the sky god from whom all the other gods had descended — eventually they had some 5,000 deities. Excavator Stephen Langdon of Oxford University made the following point:

> In my opinion, the history of the oldest religion of man has rapidly climbed from monotheism to extreme polytheism and widespread belief in evil spirits. It is in a very true sense the history of the fall of man.[8]

In *The Book of the Dead*, dealing with life and beliefs in ancient Egypt, E.A. Wallis Budge strongly makes the point that the Egyptians also originally believed in one God, with His attributes eventually being recognized as pointing to many gods. Even in the story of the Passover and the exodus from Egypt we probably see a glimmer of this. Thus, at Exodus 12:31 the pharaoh tells Moses and Aaron, "Go — serve the Lord!" The pharaoh was supposedly the living manifestation of Ra, the sun god, but he now acknowledges Jehovah!

The Sumerian King List

According to the historian Berossos, ten kings reigned between 10,800 years and 64,800 years each, and the grand total is 432,000. Apparently they are either mistranslated (wrongly presuming that a sixties system was used instead of one based on tens), or they have been grossly exaggerated. Obviously, we cannot accept these Babylonian figures as they are usually given, but when we put them alongside the Bible figures we are impressed with the conservative nature of the Bible record. However, when properly translated the Babylonian figures are, in fact, remarkably close to the Genesis figures.

Here is that Sumerian king list again. The Egyptians and Chinese also speak of kings who lived for thousands of years. The later Greeks and Romans were more conservative, suggesting 800 to 1,000 years — closer to the Bible figures. The Jewish historian Josephus had

Sumerian King List

This picture is one of three copies of the inscription on the Sumerian king list. The kings listed supposedly lived from 10,000 to 64,000 years each. The figures are clearly exaggerated or mistranslated, but this and other records make it clear that men did live for very long periods before the flood.

no doubts about the authenticity of long-living early men. The Sumerian king list suddenly reduces the reigns of the kings after the flood down to about 100 years — and we find a somewhat similar decrease in longevity in the Bible records. It is likely that the Babylonian writer of the Sumerian king list had access to the material contained in Genesis 11.

Professor Donald Wiseman states (in *Illustrations from Biblical Archaeology*),

> The lists agree with the Bible that it was the tenth who survived the great flood. WB44 reads "then the flood swept down (again) from heaven." This clear break in history is marked by a line drawn to divide the text from that describing post-diluvian events.[9]

An Ancient God? — No — Nimrod!

Of all the treasures excavated at Nineveh in ancient Assyria, none caused more surprise — and alarm! — than this massive head of Nimrod. in fact, some of the workers were terrified.

The actual site was Calah, one of the "alternative" Assyrian capitals. A new king would not be satisfied with his father's palace at (e.g.) Koujunyik, about 20 miles to the north. Several cities were administrative centers at various times — including the above two, as well as Asshur, and also Khorsabad. Nimrud (Calah) was part of "Greater Nineveh."

Calah is still referred to as "Nimrud"

Statue of Nimrod

The local workers were really afraid when they uncovered this statue of Nimrod, described in Genesis 10:9 as a mighty hunter (in that he searched for men who would obey him).

Close-up of Nimrod Statue

after the biblical Nimrod who was its founder. In modern times the city was excavated by Professor Sir Max Mallowan, the husband of mystery novel writer Agatha Christie. (She distinguished herself by her meticulous care of two highly prized gold lion ornaments, slowly adapting them to the intense high temperature of modern Iraq after being in a muddy well at Nimrud for over two centuries.)

Nimrod Again

The Temenos of Nimrod is on the slopes of Mount Nimrud in Turkey, and is about 2,200 feet above sea leavel. This is an extraordinary site, and it is considered by many to be the eighth wonder of the world. The influence of Nimrod was widespread indeed!

Nimrod — "The Mighty Tyrant"

In Genesis 10:8-9 we read:

> And Cush begat Nimrod; he began to be a mighty one in the earth.
>
> He was a mighty hunter before the Lord: Wherefore it is said, "Even as Nimrod the mighty hunter before the Lord."

Nimrod's name means, "Let us rebel!" and it seems likely that his father Cush actually trained him to be a rebel against God. Nimrod brought many of the earth's inhabitants under his sway. The *Jerusalem Targum* says,

> He was powerful in hunting and in wickedness before the Lord, for he was a hunter of the sons of men, and he said to them, "Depart from the judgment of the Lord, and adhere to the judgment of Nimrod!" Therefore it is said: "As Nimrod the strong one, strong in hunting, and in wickedness before the Lord."

Nimrod built Babylon as well as Calah (Gen. 11:4, 8-9) Genesis 10:11 should be translated that he (Nimrod) went forth from Shinar (Babylonia) into Asshur (Assyria).

The Ancient Sumerian Civilization

Genesis 11 tells of the beginning of the settlement on the Plain of Shinar, or Sumer as it is now called in secular history. Verse 2 says "they journeyed in the East." It was a literal journey, in the general area where Abraham's family lived before they migrated to the promised land of Canaan.

Then we read in Genesis 11:3-4:

> Let us make brick, and burn them thoroughly. Go to, let us build a city and a tower, whose top may reach unto heaven; let us make us a name, lest we be scattered abroad upon the face of the whole earth.

Ancient Civilization on the Plain of Shinar

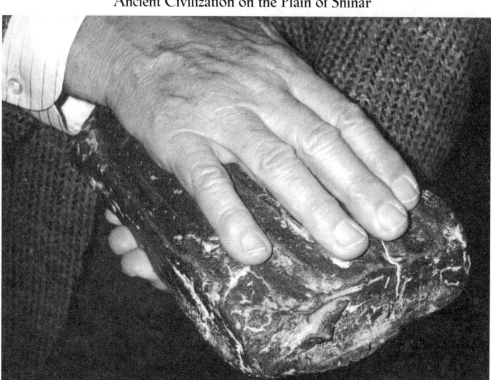

Furnaced bricks made possible the construction of the Tower of Babel.

Ancient people often built cities around their sacred towers. Sir Leonard Woolley found that at the city of Ur, and it has been found at other sites also. With the successful development of furnaced bricks, much bigger buildings were possible than with stones. So men decided to build a great tower towards heaven. Possibly they were thinking of being safe in case another flood judgment came; certainly they were setting themselves up as a super people, and their tower would not be to the glory of God. This becomes clear by the excavation of later towers. A common pattern was to have the shrine of the god at the top, as the focal point.

All sorts of sexual abominations and anti-God practices were associated with these shrines. It was little wonder that God was displeased: such temples spoke of the rejection of Him as the true God.

"Brick Instead of Stone" (Gen. 11:3)

These early Sumerians utilized a great deal of clay — cooking pots, children's toys, and even writing on clay tablets. Because of the nature of clay, the people developed the angular cuneiform style of writing, digging into the clay. The Egyptians used the papyrus reed as their basic "paper," and so they developed a cursive, flowing style as they wrote across the face of the papyrus (later known as "paper").

As our passage in Genesis 11 reminds us, they had brick instead of stone. They applied the art of furnacing and so they were now able to build much higher buildings than previously when they had been restricted to stone. Bitumen ("slime") was common in the area, and this was used as mortar.

Ancient Bricks from Sumeria

The brick on the left is sun-dried, whereas that on the right has been furnaced to about 900°F.

They did indeed "burn them thoroughly" (Gen. 11:3). These two come from the area, but at a somewhat later period. They are in the possession of the Australian Institute of Archaeology. The one on the right was taken to brickmakers in Melbourne, Australia. They reported that it had been heated to about 900°F — almost the "running" stage. Modern bricks are furnaced at a higher temperature, but these ancient bricks certainly were "burnt thoroughly."

As a matter of interest, the handmark of the man who prepared the brick on the right hand side can be seen on its upper surface. He patted it into shape before it was dispatched to the furnace, and his handmark is on the upper surface.

Babylon and the Tower of Babel

There is good reason to believe that the Tower of Babel was located in this ancient city of Babylon.

Babylon — Where the Tower of Babel Was Located

These are ruins of ancient Babylon. (Iraq's President Saddam Hussein undertook a great deal of rebuilding of the ancient administrative buildings of this site as a tourist attraction.)

In Genesis 4 there are records of Cain building a city, and there are also references to harps, organs, and the early use of metal. Despite earlier beliefs to the contrary, excavations have endorsed the general picture of such technical achievements, as at Tell Hassuna, Nineveh, Tell Chagar Bazar, and other sites.

In his *Illustrations from Biblical Archaeology*, Professor Donald Wiseman refers to a myth about the god Oannes, "the god who daily taught the newly created inhabitants of Babylonia the knowledge of writing, numbers, and arts of every kind, including agriculture, husbandry (the naming of animals), and architecture, necessary to civilized life for men living in the plain."[10]

Genesis 10 contains the remarkable "Table of Nations" which is the record of the beginnings of the nations of antiquity. Professor W.F. Albright has referred to it as "an astonishingly accurate document" and he states that "it stands absolutely alone in ancient literature, without a remote parallel even among the Greeks."

Even the story of the Tower of Babel and the confusion of languages is no longer disregarded. One recovered tablet tells about mankind being dispersed because the gods were displeased with the building that men were constructing. Mankind was dispersed overnight, and their language was confused.

Possible Site of the Tower of Babel

Some of the bricks from the possible Tower of Babel have been used to build houses in Hillah, this being a large town several miles south of Babylon.

Site of the Tower of Babel?

This large pool at modern Babylon is over the ruins of an early structure that was possibly the original Tower of Babel. Whatever the location, the fact of the dispersal from Babel and the confusion of tongues is discussed seriously by modern scholars. The American Oriental Society put out a series of essays in honor of the famous archaeologist E.A. Speiser. One essay by Professor S.N. Kramer of the University of Pennsylvania is entitled "The 'Babel of Tongues' — A Sumerian Version." Dr. Kramer reminds us that E.A. Speiser analyzed with characteristic acumen, learning, and skill the Mesopotamian background of the "Tower of Babel" narrative, and came to the conclusion that it "had a demonstrable source in cuneiform literature." Dr. Kramer wrote that his paper would "help to corroborate and confirm Speiser's conclusion by bringing to light a new parallel to one of the essential motifs in the 'Tower of Babel' theme — the confusion of tongues."

Professor Speiser was by no means alone in this view: Professor Robert Braidwood was another who referred to the present widespread acceptance that there was a factual basis to much about early civilization that had previously been regarded by many scholars as purely mythical.

Epic of Atrahasis

Since the translation of the fragmentary *Epic of Atrahasis*, it has become clear that the ancient Babylonians regarded history such as that of the creation and the flood as being continuous. It has now been put forward in secular archaeological writings that Genesis 1 through 11 are meant to be taken seriously, as the *Epic of Atrahasis* and other records touch various aspects of history recorded in the early chapters of Genesis. Another ancient record, the *Epic of Enmerkar*, has some similarity to the record of the Garden of Eden. It refers to the land of Dilmun as "a clean and bright place where the lion killed not, and the wolf snatched not the lamb." The Ebla Tablets, found in Syria in the 1970s, include Dilmun in a list of

Epic of Atrahasis

When this fragmentary epic was translated it was realized that the early chapters of Genesis were literal history. The epic was an inferior record of events such as creation and the flood.

known places. If Dilmun was an actual place, why not Eden? Perhaps Dilmun was in fact Eden! There are interesting similarities — such as no death originally, and animals living together harmoniously.

The factual nature of those chapters has been further endorsed by other tablets that seem to touch on biblical incidents. Thus, in Genesis 3 the fall of man is recorded and there is some similarity to the Babylonian "Myth of Adapa," where we have "the food of life" being similar to "the tree of life," but the origin of human sin is not envisaged. Scheming, immoral gods were certainly not involved in the creation of moral man.

Archaeology Names Kings and Rulers

Archaeology has recovered the names of many kings and rulers. In this case, kings of the First Dynasty at Babylon are listed, and then ten kings of a further dynasty are recorded down to about 1500 B.C. Records of other people are far more fragmentary than those of the Bible. Only the Hebrew people have authentic, accurate records of their earliest history. They not only date back to important dynasties, but right back to Adam, the father of us all.

The records, according to the Bible itself, were in written form — "This is the BOOK of the origins of Adam" (Gen. 2:4): it is "sepher" which means "book." Evidence from the writing styles of surrounding nations indicates that the man named at the end of the tablet would have been responsible for the tablet that ended at that point. Thus Moses was pointing to the original author when he included state-

List Naming Kings of Babylon

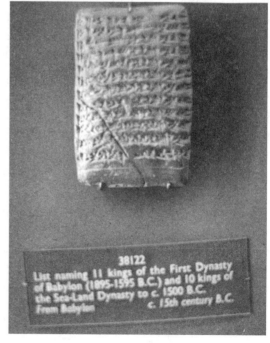

This tablet records the names of 11 kings of the First Dynasty of Babylon from 1895–1595 B.C., together with 10 kings down to about 1500 B.C. Writing was an early art.

ments such as, "These are the origins of SHEM. . . . These are the origins of TERAH. . . ." The person so named wrote from personal knowledge. (See *New Discoveries in Babylonia about Genesis* by P.J. Wiseman, revised by Professor Donald Wiseman and re-issued in *Clues to Creation in Genesis.*[11]

The tablet pictured at the bottom of page 48 gives Babylonian records of ten post-flood kings: Genesis 1 through 11 give names of leaders, preserved in written form, and dating to BEFORE the flood. No other ancient record can be compared with the preservation demonstrated in the Genesis records.

Genesis Chapters 1 Through 11: A Survey

Genesis 1, the record of creation, has surface similarities to the Babylonian epic *Enuma Elish*. However, the Babylonian epic has been corrupted and distorted through the centuries, and contains grotesque absurdities. The *Epic of Atrahasis* refers to creation and the flood, and scholars believe it points to an actual historical record (cf. Genesis).

Genesis 2, telling about the Garden of Eden, has some similarity to the *Epic of Emmerkar*. It refers to the land Dilmun, "a clean and bright place where the lion killed not, the wolf snatched not the lamb." The Ebla tablets include Dilmun in a list of places.

Genesis 3 records the fall of man. There are surface similarities in the Babylonian myth of Adapa, such as "the food of life" being similar to "the tree of life," but the origin of human sin is NOT considered. Scheming, immoral gods were not involved in the creation of perfectly moral men. Seals depicting a man, a woman, and a serpent have been found at Tepe Gawra, north of Nineveh, at Nineveh itself — the latter showing a tree also — and at Ur. They might point back to the Fall.

Genesis 4 tells of Cain building a city (Gen. 4:17). Verse 21 speaks of harps and organs, and verse 22 points to the early use of metal. Despite earlier beliefs to the contrary, excavations endorse the general picture of this chapter, as at Tell Hassuna, Nineveh, Tell Chagar Bazar, and other sites.

Genesis 5 records details of men who lived for hundreds of years. The effects of sin and disease were not as great then as now. The climate was probably dramatically different before the flood. This is hinted at in the Sumerian king list, found at ancient Kish. It tells of kings BEFORE THE FLOOD who lived for thousands of years. Those AFTER the flood lived for very much shorter periods. Recent research suggests that the Babylonian figures can be translated differently, to give figures similar to those in Genesis.

Genesis Chapters 6 to 9 record the events immediately preceding the flood, the flood itself, and the after-events. Finds such as those at Ur, Kish, and Fara indicate floods at different times — NOT the biblical flood. Genesis tells of a holy God who decreed judgment on sinful man. There is nothing grotesque as in the *Epic of Gilgamesh*.

Genesis 10 contains the remarkable "Table of Nations," the record of the beginnings of the nations of antiquity. Professor W.F. Albright referred to it as "astonishingly accurate."[12]

Genesis 11 tells of the Tower of Babel, the confusion of tongues, the dispersal of peoples, and the movement of Abraham and his family from Ur to Haran. King Ur-Nammu of Ur (2044 to 2007 B.C.) was supposedly commanded by the gods to build such a ziggurat, but a recovered tablet says it greatly offended them, so they threw it down in a night, confounded man's language, and spread people far and wide.

Genesis Chapters 1 to 11 are at times "supra-historical," beyond present historical happenings, but they record actual happenings. They are a necessary introduction to Abraham, the father of the Hebrew people, uniquely tracing ancestry to one man. This is also "the seed plot of the Bible," introducing us to great doctrines about God who is Creator, Friend, Revealer, Judge, Redeemer, Restorer, and Sustainer. These doctrines are developed in later Scriptures, but never put aside.

SECTION II:

IN THE BEGINNING GOD . . .

Pointers to Creation

The first verse of the Bible states:

In the beginning God created the heavens and the earth (Gen. 1:1).

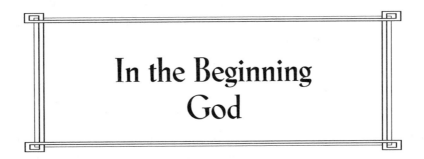

In the Beginning
God

When was "In the beginning?" Many people think that a great period of time is essential to evolution. Actually the more time available, the less likelihood there is of complex design, for *entropy* is increased with time. Thus, the possibility of meaningful design by chance is actually reduced over time. In any case, there is simply not enough time, even by the standards demanded by evolutionists for random, chance evolution, to lead to meaningful design.

The Pre-Flood Atmosphere

Some Christians (perhaps naively!) think there must be millions or billions of years for creation, for otherwise what was God doing? Such reasoning is fallacious. Whether we think of six thousand or six billion years, either figure is less than a drop of water in the great ocean of eternity. We three-dimensional earthlings cannot easily comprehend another dimension beyond time — but we certainly should not try to put God into our limited framework of time. The concept of being eternal is virtually incomprehensible to us humans, but that does not detract from its reality. God is eternal.

Today we hear a lot about radio-carbon dating, and — wrongly — millions of years. Radio carbon dating applies to only thousands, not millions, of years.

There are many other arguments that point to a recent creation — thousands rather than millions of years.

Some other methods of radio-carbon dating supposedly point to millions of years. Such dates are notoriously suspect — often because it is presumed that atmospheric conditions were the same before the flood as after. That is seriously challenged, for the partial oxygen pressure was apparently twice as great before the flood as afterwards. This means that both man and animal would have been much larger and lived much longer before the flood — as Professor Ed Blick reminds us in the following quotation:

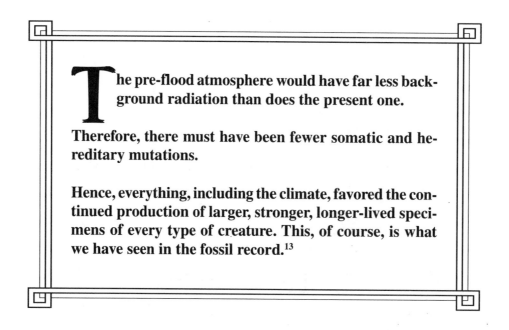

The pre-flood atmosphere would have far less background radiation than does the present one.

Therefore, there must have been fewer somatic and hereditary mutations.

Hence, everything, including the climate, favored the continued production of larger, stronger, longer-lived specimens of every type of creature. This, of course, is what we have seen in the fossil record.[13]

In addition, there is very good reason to believe that the earth was one solid mass before the flood, resting on only one tectonic plate, and the seas covered much of the land. The area covered by the earth's surface was dramatically increased, and consequently this was another factor causing that partial oxygen pressure on all creatures to be drastically reduced — it was more diffuse. Put in layman's language, there was only the same amount of oxygen pressure, but it was now spread over a much wider surface.

The Age of the Sun

The comment by solar physicist John Eddy of the High Altitude Observatory at Boulder, Colorado, indicates that supposedly outdated statements in the Bible must be taken very seriously after all:

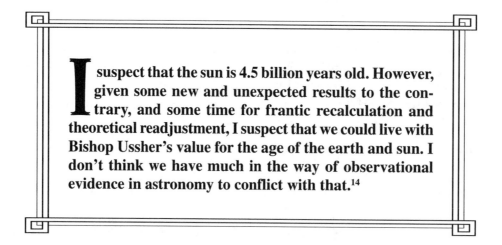

I suspect that the sun is 4.5 billion years old. However, given some new and unexpected results to the contrary, and some time for frantic recalculation and theoretical readjustment, I suspect that we could live with Bishop Ussher's value for the age of the earth and sun. I don't think we have much in the way of observational evidence in astronomy to conflict with that.[14]

Although the exact figures are a matter of controversy, it is widely accepted that the sun's size is decreasing because of the huge amount of heat it is constantly discharging. This leads to the fact that the earth cannot be billions or even millions of years old, for even 100,000 years ago the earth and the sun would have been one mass. The sun and the earth are both relatively young.

Another interesting fact is that the earth is ideally situated in relation to the sun. If we were much closer we would be shriveled up by the intense heat: if we were much further away we would be frozen by the intense cold.

The relationship of the earth to the sun points to design, and to the God who personally designed and supervised the sun as it was set in its appointed place in the heavens.

The following quotation accompanying this comment (opposite) indicates that supposedly outdated statements in the Bible must be taken very seriously after all.

The Break-up of Star Clusters

Another argument often put forward to support an "old age" for the universe relates to the ages of the galaxies in the heavens. As the following quotation by Dr. Harold S. Slusher, professor of physics and astronomy at the University of Texas, shows, measurement techniques have so increased in this generation that is now possible to estimate when the break-up of the stars began. The result has been a surprise to "establishment" astronomers.

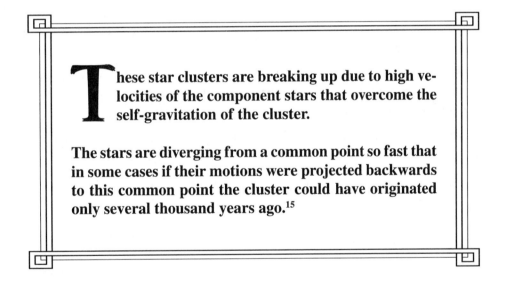

These star clusters are breaking up due to high velocities of the component stars that overcome the self-gravitation of the cluster.

The stars are diverging from a common point so fast that in some cases if their motions were projected backwards to this common point the cluster could have originated only several thousand years ago.[15]

Such sensational evidence doesn't usually make headlines for it goes against the "establishment" position. Occasionally, however, a hint of changed thinking creeps into the Press. Thus, the Melbourne (Australia) *Herald-Sun* of December 9, 1996, had a paragraph under the heading "QUOTABLE." It was a simple statement:

"This is one more factor that's got to go into the discussion of the ages of globular clusters." — U.S. astronomer Robert Kraft on a new theory that globular clusters — dense balls of stars — might be up to three billion years younger than thought.

The reduction of the age of globular clusters by three billion years is really dramatic. Once again we begin to get close to the young ages implied in the Genesis record!

When Did Stars Begin to Move Away from Each Other?

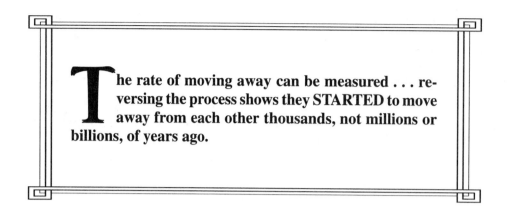

The rate of moving away can be measured . . . reversing the process shows they STARTED to move away from each other thousands, not millions or billions, of years ago.

Professor Slusher's statement about stars moving away from each other has important implications for the very origin of those stars. He states emphatically that their origin could only have been several thousand years ago.

Clearly this is dramatically different from the estimates of millions, and even billions, of years for their origin.

We are in the computer age, and as "the computer revolution" proceeds, more and more seemingly established viewpoints are being challenged.

Thus it is possible to know the rate at which the clusters of stars are moving away from each other. Astonishingly to many astronomers, when the process is reversed it becomes clear that the movement commenced only several thousand years ago.

That's in accordance with the Bible record in Genesis 1.

An Atomic Energy Scientist Comments

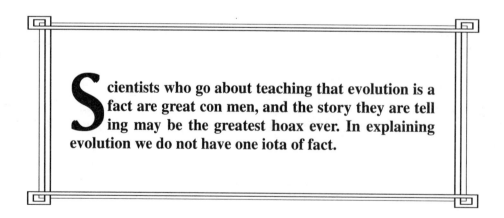

Scientists who go about teaching that evolution is a fact are great con men, and the story they are telling may be the greatest hoax ever. In explaining evolution we do not have one iota of fact.

The quotation is strong language, coming from a recognized authority with the United States Atomic Energy Commission, physiologist Dr. T.N. Tahmisian.

Who are the "con men"? Not those creationists who declare their belief in the Genesis record of creation . . . not those followers of Jesus Christ who stand with Him in believing the actuality of the literal man "Adam." Those CON MEN are scientists who go about teaching that evolution is a fact. Their story MAY BE the greatest HOAX ever. "In explaining evolution we do not have one iota of fact."

Strong words indeed!

Mythology Has Penetrated. . . .

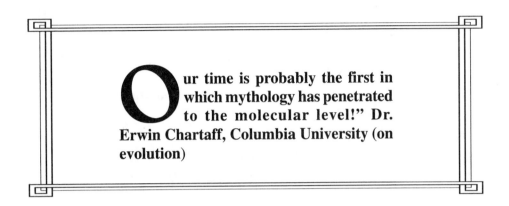

Our time is probably the first in which mythology has penetrated to the molecular level!" Dr. Erwin Chartaff, Columbia University (on evolution)

If evolution is a form of "mythology that has penetrated to the molecular level," it is not surprising to find that some leading evolutionists are prepared to face the problem objectively.

Thus Professor H.J. Lipton has written,

" . . . the only acceptable explanation is creation. . . ."

This eminent man of science was clearly not writing as a creationist! And the problem is not only recognized by physicists, for the problems for Darwinian evolution extend into many other fields of science as a plethora of many modern books has made clear.

Geologists and biologists have begun to see the problem of circular reasoning with arguments whereby the rocks date the fossils, and the fossils date the rocks.

Increasing evidence that "early" creatures and men co-existed have thrown great doubt on the authenticity of the "geological column" as a means of dating known life forms, both extant and extinct.

The symbiotic relationship between insects and plants, and even in the various components of our atmosphere, are further pointers to simultaneous creation (in maturity) rather than slowly evolving forms whereby the daughter exists before the mother — and the great, great grandchild before the ancestor him or herself.

There is increasing confusion in the camp of informed evolutionists where they are prepared to face the facts objectively.

A Fairy Tale of Evolution

Prominent French scientist Professor Louis Bounoure has stated, "Evolution is a fairy tale for grown-ups," — and similar quotes could be given from other leading scientists.

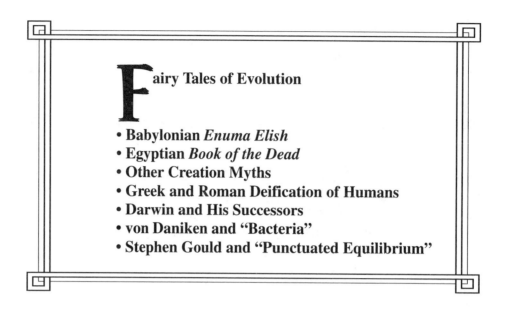

Fairy Tales of Evolution

- **Babylonian *Enuma Elish***
- **Egyptian *Book of the Dead***
- **Other Creation Myths**
- **Greek and Roman Deification of Humans**
- **Darwin and His Successors**
- **von Daniken and "Bacteria"**
- **Stephen Gould and "Punctuated Equilibrium"**

The Darwinian "Theory of Evolution" is not the first such "fairy tale." The early Babylonians had their epic *Enuma Elish*, with the god Marduk cutting the crocodile goddess Tiamat in half, making heaven from one half and earth from the other. The Egyptian *Book Of the Dead* started with monotheism (belief in one God) but soon showed how crude polytheism (belief in more than one god) had taken over.

The Greeks and the Romans had many grotesque deities, including man himself. Their concept was of gods made in the likeness of man — the opposite of Genesis 1, which speaks of man made uniquely in the image of God.

Evolution Is a Fairy Tale!

Leaders in the field of anthropology and palaeontology constantly change their mind as the evidence shows that their ideas based on Darwinian theory do not stand the test of their own empirical evidence.

Thus there are many statements such as this one from Lyall :

> Not surprisingly, despite the diligent research done in East Africa by palaeontologist Richard Leakey and Donald Johanson, there are gaping holes in the evolutionary record, some of them extending for four to six million years. Modern apes, for instance, seem to have sprung out of nowhere. They have no yesterday, no fossil record. And the true origin of humans — of upright, naked, toolmaking, big-brained beings — is, if we are to be honest with ourselves, an equally mysterious matter.[16]

Eric von Daniken (of *Chariots of the Gods*) had "space gods" finding monkey-like creatures on a planet as they approached earth, and used "bacteria" to transform them into "homo sapiens"! That is yet another "fairy tale for grown-ups" — yet von Daniken's books have sold by the tens of millions (as personally told to me by von Daniken at the time of a four-hour debate at the University at Fargo, North Dakota).

Punctuated Equilibrium — Another Fairy Tale !

Now comes Harvard's Stephen Gould (and others) with the nonsensical "Punctuated Equilibrium" argument — a revival of the "Hopeful Monster" theory that was propounded earlier in this century. It argues for sudden bursts of activity after many thousands of years of "status quo." Suddenly a new life form bursts forth — and of course there must be two of them, of opposite sex, finding each other within their fertilization periods, being able to produce offspring — and so much more.

All this, of course, had to happen for all the vast multitudes of different species. Even the evolutionists long ago are nowhere near enough time for all this to happen.

Once again, this is "A Fairy Tale for Grown-Ups" — yet it is being seriously taught as the evolution theory to replace the admittedly out-dated Darwinian theory!

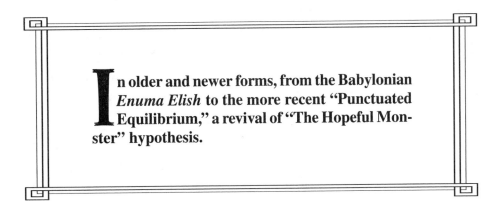

In older and newer forms, from the Babylonian *Enuma Elish* to the more recent "Punctuated Equilibrium," a revival of "The Hopeful Monster" hypothesis.

Man's Three Distinctives

Man is unique in many ways besides the three listed in the quotation below. However, these are deliberately chosen from archaeology because that is the background for this series.

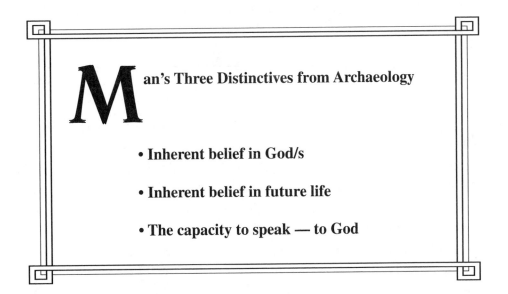

Man's Three Distinctives from Archaeology

• **Inherent belief in God/s**

• **Inherent belief in future life**

• **The capacity to speak — to God**

Despite all wishful thinking of so-called atheists, man has an inherent belief in a god or gods, and that has been demonstrated in culture after culture, across the ages. He makes images of the gods — in wood, in stone, in clay, and in many other forms. No animal does that — only man. He is declaring his belief in a higher power whom he is determined to find, if only to appease rather than to worship as with Christian belief.

Secondly, only man makes any preparation for a life to come, beyond the grave. He often embalms the bodies of departed loved ones, and buries his dead. No animal buries its dead: this is the unique declaration of man that somehow, somewhere there is life beyond the grave. So ancient peoples put food, weapons, wooden servants marked as to their future service, clothing, and even furniture — all for the next life. Man, who is made in the image of God, searches for that God, believing that he himself has a spark of eternity within himself.

Thirdly, man is essentially different from all other creatures in the matter of true speech/language. There are 16 recognized design features in true speech/language, and only man has all 16. This has compared and contrasted 26 primary and secondary features of language in humans and chimpanzees.[17] Where a feature is primary for humans (as with hearing), it is secondary for chimpanzees: where it is primary for chimpanzees, it is secondary for humans. The differences are of KIND, not of DEGREE.

And the ultimate of true speech/language is PRAYER, whereby mankind can uniquely communicate with the Creator in whose image he is created.

Ape-like Ancestors Have Slipped Away!

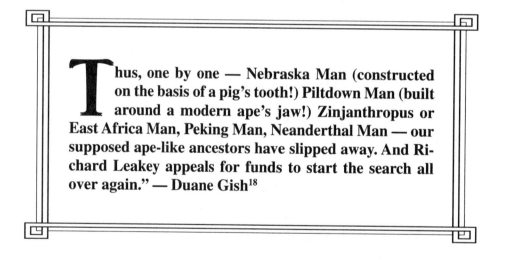

Thus, one by one — Nebraska Man (constructed on the basis of a pig's tooth!) Piltdown Man (built around a modern ape's jaw!) Zinjanthropus or East Africa Man, Peking Man, Neanderthal Man — our supposed ape-like ancestors have slipped away. And Richard Leakey appeals for funds to start the search all over again." — Duane Gish[18]

Anthropology cannot prove evolution. Piltdown Man, Nebraska Man, Neanderthal Man, Java Man, and many others have fallen by the wayside.

Geology cannot prove evolution: the finding of index fossils such as the coelocanth fish and the trilobite in "wrong strata" have thrown the seemingly assured results of geology into confusion.

Polystrate fossils — such as trees upside down and extending through, literally, dozens of strata have pointed conclusively to one great catastrophe, and not many.

It has been recognized that the fossils have been used to date the rocks, and the rocks have been used to date the fossils: such circular reasoning is quite "unscientific."

Similar evidence can be produced from other sciences such as astronomy, biology, botany, linguistics, paleontology, and physics.

Another "Baffling Limb"

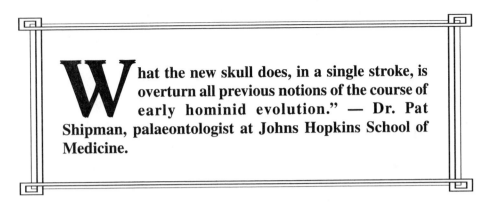

"What the new skull does, in a single stroke, is overturn all previous notions of the course of early hominid evolution." — Dr. Pat Shipman, palaeontologist at Johns Hopkins School of Medicine.

Professor Pat Shipman writes as a member of the Richard Leakey team — he being the director of the National Museum of Kenya. An editorial comment in the September 1986 edition of *Discovery* reports on the finding of a new skull:

An ancient and confounding skull, with enormous teeth, massive crests, and a tiny brain, has cast the pre-human lineage into disarray." Pat Shipman herself tells us, "What the new skull does, in a single stroke, is overturn all previous notions of the course of early hominid evolution.

Pat Shipman's article in that journal is entitled, "Baffling Limb on the Family Tree." She discusses the views of Donald Johanson, Richard Leakey, and others — and shows that previous ideas of the order of ancient skulls must be put aside. She tells us,

And then where is the ancestral hominid species? The best answer we can give right now is that we no longer have a very clear idea of who gave rise to whom; we don't know who didn't. This uncomfortable state of affairs can be summarized in three simple statements: (1) **Robustus** didn't evolve into **boisei**. (2) **Africanus** didn't evolve into **boisei**. (3) **Boisei** didn't evolve into either **africanus** or **robustus**. In fact, we don't even know what sort of ancestral species we're looking for.

Towards the end of the article she acknowledged, "It's a new era in paleoanthropology. The things we thought we understood reasonably well, we don't."

A Startling Conclusion

The last paragraph is startling. Paleontologist Pat Shipman tells us:

We need new fossils more than ever, as well as a re-examination of our old ideas. I don't think the new synthesis will come quickly, for most of these choices will make many of the primary researchers in this field uncomfortable. Changing your ideas is more painful than moving house, but the results are also more exciting. No better argument can be made to support the time, trouble, and cost of field work than this new skull. Like an earthquake, the new skull has reduced our nicely organized constructs to a rubble of awkward, sharp-edged new hypotheses. It's a sure sign of scientific progress.

Like an earthquake. . . . Scientific progress!

The fact is, it is yet another indication that the theory of evolution is in desperate disarray, drastically discredited.

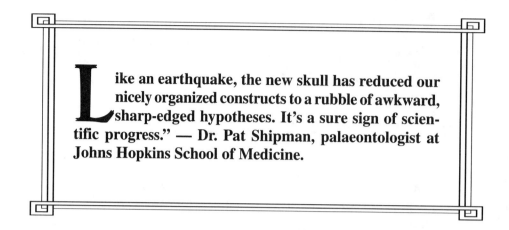

"**Like an earthquake, the new skull has reduced our nicely organized constructs to a rubble of awkward, sharp-edged hypotheses. It's a sure sign of scientific progress.**" — Dr. Pat Shipman, palaeontologist at Johns Hopkins School of Medicine.

Where Does Faith Fit In?

Evolutionists are recognizing that "FAITH" is required to support their arguments:

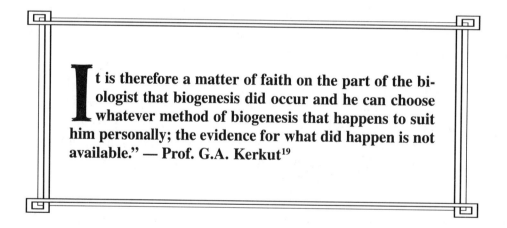

"**It is therefore a matter of faith on the part of the biologist that biogenesis did occur and he can choose whatever method of biogenesis that happens to suit him personally; the evidence for what did happen is not available.**" — Prof. G.A. Kerkut[19]

Professor G.A. Kerkut's statement is clear as to the fact that Darwinian evolution really answers nothing.

This is not an isolated opinion. Well-known philosopher and linguist Noam Chonsky has made the point that "straight line evolution" (which means only one line from an amoeba to a man) does not explain the development of true speech/language in humans. He suggests we can call it evolution if we like, but it explains nothing. Dr. Michael Denton (not a creationist) has written the challenging, *Evolution: A Theory in Crisis*. He points to the dramatic complexity of a single human cell — it is more complex in design than all the design involved in a city such as New York or London.

These are not impassioned pleas for the acceptance of creation, but an honest appraisal by scholars with very high qualifications in their fields.

As Professor Kerkut writes from a non-creationist perspective, "The evidence for what did happen is not available." And as our quotation shows, "faith is involved in a personal decision as to what method of biogenesis should be accepted."

The creationist has no such problem; he accepts the record in Genesis — the Almighty God spoke and creation took place.

Evolutionists Need Fantastic Faith

The information stored in one human cell is awesome. How did it get there? To believe that all this is the result of nothing more than blind chance is an exercise in foolishness. It means that the facts have not been logically faced.

Indeed, that is true with very many areas of the creation/evolution controversy. Take that often-quoted chicken. It starts as just a small embryo inside its mother's body, but the implanted design is incredibly complex — way beyond the possibility of "merely chance evolution."

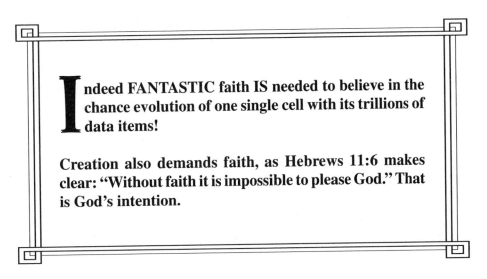

Indeed FANTASTIC faith IS needed to believe in the chance evolution of one single cell with its trillions of data items!

Creation also demands faith, as Hebrews 11:6 makes clear: "Without faith it is impossible to please God." That is God's intention.

If evolution is fact, how are questions like these answered by these embryo when they are first locked inside a shell which is itself inside its mother's body:

1. Where did it get the idea of feet?

2. What about wings — did the chicken somehow first experiment with half a wing to see if it would work? Or did it see this as being irrational and so started with one whole wing? If so, how did it know about flight, anyway?

3. What about eyes? Did it have some way of seeing through its enclosing eggshell and realize it must manufacture some eyes before leaving home — the shell, of course?

4. Then there was the voice apparatus — no self-respecting chicken would be without a voice-box. How did this wily little chicken stumble on to the highly complex system of animal communication?

5. And, of course, there are all those extras which we have not mentioned — they must be explained if we really want to understand the thinking patterns of these little chickens. They are able to cope much better than the human baby which is after all quite helpless for some time after birth.

Obviously the chicken did NOT plan all this — nor the way the digestive system works, and the heart, and the liver, and all those other organs that make up the total chicken.

The explanation involves FAITH in the living, all-powerful God, and not blind dependence on the worthless system of chance evolution.

How Do We Go from Y TO Z?

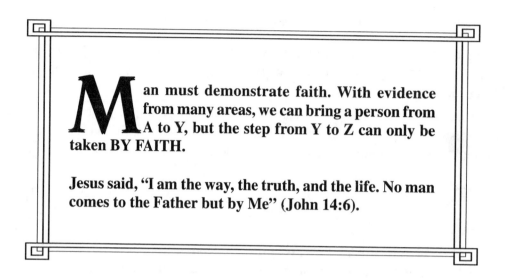

Man must demonstrate faith. With evidence from many areas, we can bring a person from A to Y, but the step from Y to Z can only be taken BY FAITH.

Jesus said, "I am the way, the truth, and the life. No man comes to the Father but by Me" (John 14:6).

Man must demonstrate faith. God demands it — for He who comes to God must believe that He IS, and is a rewarder of those who diligently seek Him (Heb. 11:6).

As our verse shows, Jesus is the way — and we can come to the Father only by Him. We need to recognize and acknowledge that we have failed — we have sinned. We ask for forgiveness of our sins, and He gives us eternal life (John 3:16; Rom. 3:23, 6:23; Eph. 2:8–10).

Here is a prayer that can lead to salvation through Jesus Christ:

> Lord Jesus Christ, I'm a sinner in need of salvation. You died on the Cross to give me salvation. I come to You now, asking You to forgive my sins and to come into my life. So, forgive me my sin, come into my life, and help me to live a life pleasing to You from this day onward. Amen.

Why not pray that prayer, meditating on it, going over it, and sincerely praying it. Jesus says, "I will not cast out the one who comes to me" (John 6:37).

He means it — take Him at His word!

SECTION III

ABRAHAM: HIS BACKGROUND AND HIS FAMILY

Schoolhouse at Ur

In the social life of ancient Ur, boys were expected to go to school. There was a schoolhouse at Abraham's city of Ur. Writing was a common art by then. Thousands of clay tablets have been found at various centers, dating approximately to his time. These include the ancient Amorite mound of Tell Ell-Harari (Mari), the ancient Hattusas (the modern Boghazkoy), Kish, and Ur itself.

Most of the cities associated with Abraham in the Bible are now known, either from archaeology or from historical records. They turn out to be important centers at the time when he lived. They were not all thriving at later times, and the local color and timing of the Bible narratives are remarkable. These were not campfire stories that grew in the telling, as earlier critics had claimed!

Abraham's City of Ur

Sir Leonard Woolley reported that he had found mud deposits from Noah's flood, with evidence of civilization, under eight feet of sterile mud. However, he found this evidence in only two of the five shafts that he sank. The evidence he found was of a flood that did not even destroy all of Ur, let alone the whole world.

In any case, similar flood evidences have been found at other sites in ancient Assyria and Babylonia — Nineveh, Erech, Kish, Nippur, and Tell Farah. These floods were separated by centuries: clearly they were not the biblical flood — for God said He would never again send such a flood as that which destroyed the whole earth in the days of Noah (Gen. 9:11).

The Genesis description of the flood clearly indicates a worldwide happening. A careful reading of the text makes that abundantly clear — even the tops of the high hills were covered (Gen. 7:19). If this was just a flood involving the Tigris-Euphrates basin, Noah and his family could have escaped over the land without the huge task of building the ark. It was clearly worldwide, and all life on earth was destroyed (Gen. 7:21–23).

Abraham's City of Ur

This man with a rifle was a guard at the site of Abraham's ancient city of Ur. He proudly told of his earlier career as a worker for Sir Leonard Woolley, the famous English excavator of this site.

Golden Vessels from Ur

The findings in the royal death pits at Ur indicated that the craftsmen of the city were very capable. The workmanship was magnificent, with golden vessels, jewelry and ornaments, golden daggers, and even a golden helmet. These findings demonstrated a remarkably advanced culture. When we remember that this was over 2,000 years before the time of our Lord on earth, we realize that so-called "primitive men" were not so primitive after all. Man has always been intelligent, with remarkable technical ability.

These electroplated copies of the golden vessels are in the museum of the Australian Institute of Archaeology. (I was director of that Institute for some years.) Notice the name "Queen Shubad" — translators now refer to her as Queen Pu-Abi.

Nonsensical arguments have been made in recent years about helmets supposedly worn by ancient astronauts who visited earth from other planets. Such helmets — so the argument goes — could not have been made by mere humans with limited intelligence and primitive technology. The golden helmet in this picture is well-established as a man-made artifact, dating to the third millennium B.C. — it had nothing to do with astronauts!

Royal Tombs of Ur

These are replicas of golden vessels found in the tomb of Queen Pu-Abi (previously translated as Shub-Ad) and Prince Mes-Kalam-Dug. The originals were excavated by Sir Leonard Woolley.

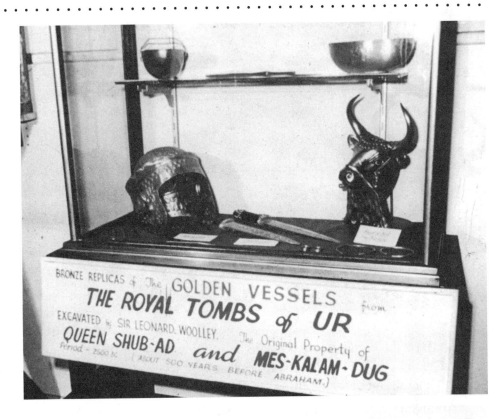

A Fluted Golden Goblet

Golden vessels were found in the tombs of royalty. Such vessels would hardly have been used by the "everyday" people.

When a royal personage died, apparently servants went down in the funeral procession into the tomb, took up their places around their departed master or mistress, and drank poison from a vessel such as this fluted golden goblet.

Apparently they believed that thereby they would have a better resurrection. No animal or bird has ever made preparations for a life to come. Nor have they ever buried their dead. Only man, made in the image of God who is eternal, has any concept of a life beyond the grave, and so in various cultures we find that preparations were made for that life. At Ur it included the provision of golden vessels for the king, queen, or prince, with servants ready to die in order to continue their life of service in the hereafter.

Man is made in the image of God Who is eternal and these people had vague ideas of pleasing the gods and ensuring a better hereafter as they went to their death.

It is believed that the servants who went in the funeral procession with their departed king, queen or princess, would have taken poison from vessels such as this. They believed they would have a better hereafter. Only humans have this belief in life after death.

Fluted Bowl from Ur

65

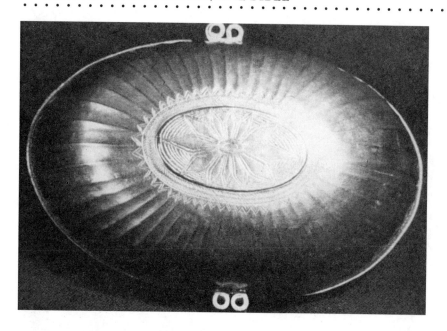

Bottom Side of Golden Fluted Dish from Ur

Only the best was good enough for a royal prince as he took his journey into the hereafter. Even that part which only sat on the table had to be constructed with careful precision.

Another Golden Vessel from Ur

This also is one of the golden vessels from Ur. The underneath side is shown in this picture, and the workmanship on that part which simply sits on the shelf or table is just as carefully wrought as the other parts of the golden vessel. Only the best was good enough for this royal prince of Ur. These findings in the royal death pits demonstrate the magnificent culture of which these people were capable.

Abraham was challenged to leave it all behind him. God is not interested in wealth and culture, and Abraham accepted that challenge to go out and to be a pilgrim and a stranger, leaving the magnificence of Ur behind him, but walking in the presence of God. Like Moses at a later time, he chose the presence of Christ, together with its reproach, rather than the magnificence of the culture that was dedicated to false gods.

In the case of Abraham, the evil worship was especially associated with the false god Nannar, the moon god; with Moses the Pharaoh himself was supposedly the manifestation of Ra the sun god.

Golden Earrings from Ur

It used to be argued that when Abraham sent his servant to find a bride for Isaac, the servant could not have taken with him the gold and silver jewelry that the Bible claims (see Gen. 24:22). However, at Ur

Golden Jewelry from Ur

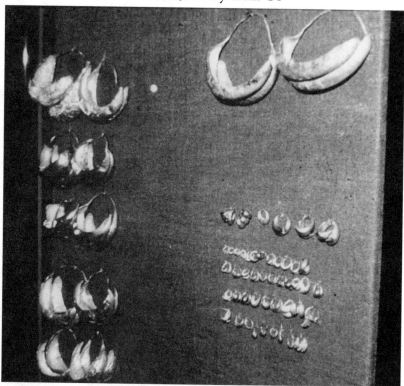

Critics said that the servant of Abraham could not have had golden earrings so early. These ones before Abraham's time are more than twice the size of those in the Genesis record.

these golden earrings were found, dating well before the time of Abraham. They are about twice the size of those that are referred to in the Bible story. The servant certainly could have carried large golden earrings as presents.

This is the sort of background material which caused the late Professor William Foxwell Albright to write as long ago as 1962:

> During the past 15 years it has become possible to pinpoint the background of the stories of Abraham (Gen. 12 through 24) with a precision wholly undreamed of when the first edition of this survey was written.[20]

Professor Albright was prepared to acknowledge the integrity of the biblical text, despite the skepticism of his earlier years.

Jewelry from Ur

This beautiful jewelry also came from the royal death pits at Ur. Some of it is in lovely gold leaf, and there are various other forms of jewelry, including silver and lapis lazulai. It was delightful workmanship, and in this case it was especially associated with Queen Pu-Abi who had died and was buried in the royal vaults. It clearly reminds us of the fact that craftsmanship in metal was well-established in the city of Ur well before the times of Abraham.

This jewelry would be appreciated and valued even by modern ladies today and of course much of it is now almost priceless. In the early chapters of Genesis we read of artificers, and the further back we go with archaeological findings, the more impressed we are that the Bible writings must be taken at face value. These necklaces date before patriarchal times, and similar finds have been made throughout the ages in ancient and modern civilizations.

As soon as settled civilization was established, people demonstrate that they have technological capacities way ahead of what many scholars of a generation ago believed was possible. Excavator Sir Leonard Woolley suggested that we must considerably revise our opinions of the standard of culture at Ur.

Gold and Silver Ornaments from Ur

A large amount of beautiful jewelry was found in the tomb of Queen Pu-Abi, some of it gold, silver, and lapis lazuli. It was remarkably "modern," much more advanced than was believed to be possible in early civilizations dating to before the time of Abraham.

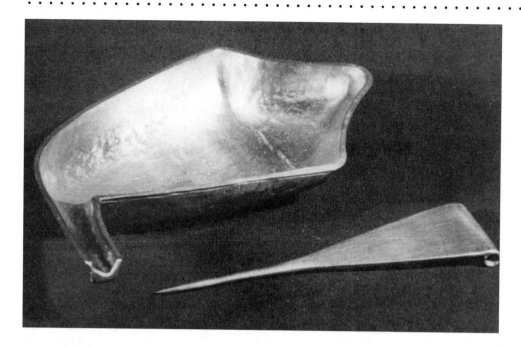

Golden Lamp Bowl and Hairpin

Queen Pu-Abi must be able to see her way in the hereafter, so this golden dish would be filled with oil to ensure she had clear light. The golden hairpin was typical of her lifetime of luxury.

Oil Lamp and Hairpin

In this case, again from the royal death pits at Ur, we have an oil lamp and a hairpin from the tomb of the departed Queen Pu-Abi. Surely in the life to come they would need a light to show the way! So a golden vessel in which oil could be placed was to accompany the queen. And she would need beautiful ornaments, so this golden hairpin was another reminder that she would be well looked after in the hereafter.

It is worth repeating that only humans had this concept of life beyond the grave and so they made what preparations they could. Oil lamps, food, weapons, and other articles used in this life were often buried with the deceased person. Man is constantly searching for the true God. The Bible makes it clear that there is indeed a life beyond the grave, and that "whosoever will" can know the reality of eternal life through coming to Him who shed His blood to give them forgiveness of sins. Thus we put our trust in Him who says, "I am the way, the truth and the life. No man comes to the Father but by Me" (John 14:6).

The practical and the beautiful were combined, with results that would be acceptable even to fastidious 20th century "moderns."

A Donkey on Chariot Rings

A Donkey on Chariot Rings

This golden donkey was mounted on the chariot rings of the queen's chariot found in those death pits at Ur. Notice that it is in fact a donkey, not a horse. It is believed that the horse was domesticated in Egypt some hundreds of years after the time of Abraham, and it is interesting to know that in his time the horse was referred to as "the wild ass of the East."

Bible references to iron are not out of place as critics had claimed.

The first mention of the horse in the Bible is in the story of Joseph, in Genesis 47:17. There we read that Joseph gave the Egyptian people bread when they delivered their horses to him. The local color of the Bible story is sustained in this seemingly casual and yet accurate mention of the horse.

The chariot rings themselves were made of iron — over 1,000 years before the so-called "Iron Age." We read in Genesis 4:22 that Tubal-Cain was "an instructor of every artificer in brass and iron." Iron was much more plentiful in the (later) Iron Age, but it certainly was used to some extent in much earlier times. These days it is recognized that some of the "ages" commonly put forward are not as clear-cut as was formerly believed.

Lyre from Ur

This is a harp (or lyre) from Ur. Once again, critics claimed that harps and other well-developed musical instruments were not known as early as Abraham's time. In fact, it was claimed that David (about 1,000 years later) could not have played on an instrument of ten strings because there were no such harps known so early.

Harp (Lyre) from Royal Death Vaults at Ur

Higher critics had formerly claimed that King David could not have had an instrument of 10 strings because such instruments were not known as early as his time. This harp from Ur, dating to over 1,000 years before David's time, actually had 13 strings.

The harp is reconstructed, but it is reconstructed in exactly the same pattern that was shown by the findings themselves in the royal death pits at Ur. Some of the artifacts had actually become part of the collapsed walls which then encased them. Reconstruction (but obviously not re-use) was possible. The places for setting the 13 strings were visible. At times there were more than 10 strings: clearly the criticisms about David playing on an instrument of 10 strings were unfounded. There are very many of these casual references to Bible backgrounds and customs. They come together as convincing evidence of the integrity of the Bible writers.

Several of these lyres were found in the royal death pits at Ur. Clearly this was not just one harp out of time as it were.

Music was established as a means of human entertainment well before the days of Abraham. A golden goat head formed part of the lyre, again reminding us of the magnificent workmanship of these people, even before the time of Abraham.

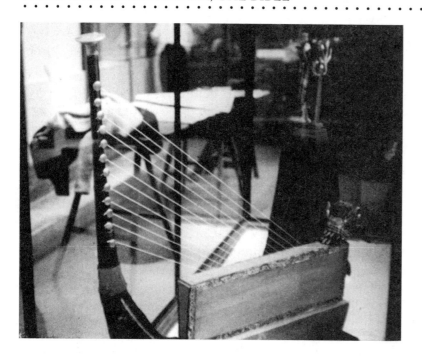

Another Lyre from Ur

There were several of these magnificent lyres. This one is reconstructed, as in the days of Ur's glory.

Another Lyre from Ur

Here is another magnificent lyre from Abraham's ancient city. As this was buried in the tombs of royalty it is interesting to ask if members of the royal family themselves played on such beautiful instruments.

The view is heightened by the fact that items buried in tombs were specifically for use in the life beyond the grave. We have already seen that such preparations were made uniquely by humans — no animal or bird even buried its dead, let alone burying food, furniture, or other provisions for the next life.

Such a practice pointed to man's inherent belief that there would be life after death. However, the only real knowledge of that life is found in the Bible — eternal life is available through Jesus who said, "No man comes to the Father except through Me" (John 14:6).

Golden Goat's Head from Ur

This particular golden goat's head was on another lyre from Ur. Its magnificence again reminds us of the glory of Ur, even well before the times of Abraham. It fits the general pattern in early Genesis of men being capable as artisans.

The picture at Genesis 4:21-22 is even earlier than the civilization at Ur, for it is pre-flood. There we read of Jubal who was "the father of all who handle the harp and the organ" and of Tubal-Cain who was "an instructor of every artificer in brass and iron."

The excavators were surprised at the advanced technology at Ur, but man was created by God in His own image. The clues both as to man's technical and musical interests are clearly given in early Genesis. Those records are factual history.

Some "modern" writers have suggested that these

A Golden Goat's Head

This stylized golden goat's head formed part of one of the several lyres found in the royal death pits at Ur. It is another reminder of the luxury associated with the city from which Abraham migrated.

records were first compiled after the time of Solomon. However, the records consistently point to eye-witness recording. Over and over again that touch of the eyewitness is demonstrated in the Genesis records.

Royal Standard from Ur

These members of nobility are celebrating while drinking beer and listening to music.

Royal Standard from Ur

This pictorial mosaic standard was made of beautiful lapis lazulai and shell, and it comes from Ur of the Chaldees, Abraham's ancient city. Professor Donald Wiseman writes about this royal standard:

> A prince feasts with courtiers and receives booty from the enemy. This is a master-piece of Sumerian art.[21]

Notice that the man second from the right at the top is holding an ancient harp. Human nature changes little, and recovered artifacts and paintings demonstrate that people loved their music and their art forms right through the ages.

It did not take hundreds or even dozens of generations to pass before music and art forms were developed. Man was created as an intelligent being by God, and evidences of his intelligence are shown in excavation after excavation.

A School in Patriarchal Times

These stone benches were excavated at the city of Mari. It is believed that they formed part of a schoolhouse — probably similar to the one at Ur.

Stone Seats at Mari

These are seats — actually stone benches — at the ancient city of Mari. It is possible that the little bowls were receptacles in which counters could be put. Certainly writing was an established art, with schools relatively common, back in patriarchal times.

Mari is of interest because of some aspects indirectly touching the Bible. In "Archaeology in Bible Lands", Howard F. Vos writes that the documents recovered from Mari contained names equivalent to some mentioned in Genesis 11:16, 23, 24, and 27 (e.g. Peleg, Serug, Nahor), thus showing they were historical names (but not the actual biblical persons). "Moreover they mention customs reflected in the patriarchal narratives and throw light on the tribal organization and traditions of Syria in patriarchal times."[22]

We notice in passing that these and many other writings answer the criticisms of a generation ago that Moses, who lived centuries after Abraham, could not have written. Such claims have been shown to be nonsense. However, critics do not give up easily and they claimed that even if Moses could write, he would not have known law codes. Law codes were then found, and so it was claimed that Moses merely copied other people's law codes. However, it was then shown that the code of Moses, given by inspiration of God, was dramatically superior to other codes, especially in areas of spiritual values.

Pythagoras' Theorem at Ur

This is a clay tablet from Abraham's city of Ur. It does not actually give Pythagoras' theorem in its stated terms — that in a right-angled triangle the square on the hypotenuse is equal to the sum of the squares on the other two sides. However, it does give figures (which can be seen at the top of the tablet) demonstrating that the principle of that particular theorem was known something like 1,500 years before the time of the Greek mathematician Pythagoras. This knowledge would have been useful for the construction of buildings, etc.

Over and over again we find that things that were supposedly understood only many centuries later than the dates claimed by Bible writers were in fact known to "ancient" people.

There never was such a thing as a primitive people in the sense of half-man, half-ape, developing into an intelligent state over vast periods of time. Instead we find evidence that as soon as civilization is there, mankind is intelligent, often with highly developed writing skills, always with complex language, and so much more.

Early Form of Pythagoras' Theorem at Ur

The principles of Pythagoras' theorem were known and used in building constructions.

Ziggurat at Ur

This ziggurat or temple tower at Ur was excavated by Sir Leonard Woolley. There were also about 2,000 temple employees spinning, weaving, keeping accurate records, and initiating trade.

The Ziggurat (Temple Tower) at Ur

About a quarter of the city's religion was given over to various temples, the most important being the ziggurat (temple tower) of the moon god Nannar, also known as Sin — no connection with our modern word "sin." The great blot on the culture of Ur was in association with their religion. The records about their ziggurat showed that their worship included all sorts of abominations in connection with ritual offerings to the moon god.

It is probable that the ziggurats were originally intended as a challenge to God. The Jewish historian Josephus says that Nimrod was a declared antagonist of the Lord, and arranged for the building of the Tower of Babel so that he and others could be safe even if God did visit the earth with another flood. This would explain why, both in the bible and in the Babylonian record, God was angry at such activity and destroyed the offensive building.

Other people possibly followed Nimrod's open defiance, for ziggurat-type buildings are known in a number of "old-world" countries.

In addition to religious ceremonies, in this massive structure thousands of women were employed, spinning and weaving, and the trade extended internationally. A surprisingly modern system of bookkeeping was maintained, with records as to the totals incoming and outgoing, and the amounts owing to and by various customers in the land itself and beyond.

Many Shrines to False Gods

The main worship center at Ur was the ziggurat dedicated to the moon god Nannar, but there were many other shrines. The appeasing of the awe-inspiring gods was important, and the priests had great control over the lives of these people in their spiritual bondage.

The hero Gilgamesh (of "flood" fame) is depicted as praying to Sin (i.e. Nannar) when "I saw lions and grew afraid." In the *Mythological Descent of Ishtar to the Nether World*, the goddess Ishtar (Asherah) is referred to as "the daughter of Sin" (Nannar). In later Assyrian times the ruthless Assyrian King Ashur-Nasir-

Ur Ziggurat and Other Buildings

Ruins of some of the temples at Ur are pictured in this scene.

Pal (883–859 B.C.) recognized both Sin and Shamash as the light-giving gods.[23] Sin/Nannar was clearly a prominent deity in Old Testament times.

Nannar was both king and god at Ur in Abraham's time, while his consort was the goddess Nin-Gal. There was a special moon god ritual associated with the city. The top level of the ziggurat ("the hill of heaven") was given over to temple rituals.

Chapels for worship were found in residential areas of the city (in addition to those in the general area of the ziggurat). As well as commercial income from trading activities, tithes were paid by the people for the support of the priests and the religious establishment.

The Moon God Nannar

The moon god Nannar as pictured at Abraham's city of Ur. His name is sometimes given as "SIN."
That has no connection with our modern word but it is strangely appropriate.

The Moon God Nannar

This is the moon god Nannar who was worshiped in the city of Ur. He was also worshiped at Haran, for they were sister cities. Abraham's father Terah went from Ur to Haran, but did not move on into the Promised Land. Abraham himself (and his family and servants) also stayed in Haran.

At the end of Joshua's life he made a great, challenging speech to the people of Israel, urging them as follows:

> Choose you this day whom you will serve; whether the gods which your fathers served that were on the other side of the flood [= River Euphrates], or the gods of the Amorites, in whose land you dwell: but as for me and my house, we will serve the Lord (Josh. 24:15)

This indicates that Abraham's ancestors on the other side of the Euphrates served gods such as Nannar. When Terah moved from Ur to Haran, it seems he was prepared to move only from one center of moon worship to another. Abraham waited in Haran until his father Terah died: possibly he should have moved out to the land of promise much earlier. The Lord in His grace renewed the call to Abraham at Haran, and Abraham obeyed (Gen. 12:1–5).

A Woman Brought Before the Moon God at Ur

This depicts a woman being brought before the moon god Nannar.

A Woman Is Taken Before the Moon God

Every woman in Ur was supposed to offer herself at least once in her lifetime to the priests of the moon god Nannar. This could be arranged by substitution, paying one of the temple prostitutes to undertake this activity.

The practices associated with the worship of Nannar were abominable to God — and no doubt to Abraham. Not only were there "sacred prostitutes" at the temple, but there were also homosexual men, holding office specifically for the offering of their bodies to the priests.

The alternative name of "Sin" was strangely appropriate for Nannar the moon god. The word is not the same as our modern word "sin," but the practices were indeed sinful. The judgment of God is declared at Romans 1: 21–32: "God gave them up" (verses 24, 26, 28).

The wickedness of Sodom is also shown in the context of homosexual activity (see Gen. 19:1–13). Love for the sinner does not mean endorsement of his sinful practices.

The Setting Sun at Ur

The setting sun throwing Ur's ancient ziggurat into shadow reminds us that Abraham's city was losing its glory. Abraham was called to be a pilgrim — but walking in the presence of God.

Abraham the Nomad

We have seen that in Abraham's early life he was associated with the city of Ur with its magnificent culture, but that he was challenged to leave it and to be a pilgrim and a stranger, walking in the presence of God. Abraham would have lived in tents not unlike those utilized by modern nomads — but not with the television enjoyed by many Bedouin today!

Apart from the cave of Machpelah, purchased from the sons of Heth so that Sarah could be buried (Gen. 23), there is no record of Abraham ever owning any land. He moved around and he was much freer to do so than would have been the case in the time of his grandson Jacob. By then the relatively clear lands were becoming increasingly occupied.

Abraham was rich, but he did not know the luxury of settling down into any one comfortable house. He looked for a city whose builder and maker was God (Heb. 11:10).

When he left the magnificence of Ur and later of Haran it was because he chose to accept the promises of God, promises that were to be fulfilled in a life beyond the grave. True morality had departed from Ur, and this setting sun on the ziggurat is a fitting reminder that its passing glory soon departed.

The Fertile Crescent

The Fertile Crescent — named as such by the famous Professor J.H. Breasted — is so called because the territory referred to is in fact a fertile crescent, running around the great Arabian Desert. It runs up between the two Rivers Euphrates and Tigris, down through Syria into Israel, and across into Egypt.

This is the general area over which Abraham traveled. His journey from Ur to Haran and then into Israel would have taken some months, with sheep moving at perhaps three miles a day. The geographic clues given in the patriarchal records fit the times. Thus, when Abraham journeyed, the possibilities for moving freely were much greater than even in the later

This is the area over which Abraham moved as he set out from Ur for Canaan.

days of Isaac. By then territorial claims were more definite.

The different areas were even more settled in the time of Jacob. Archaeology has demonstrated that there were more and more territorial changes as various peoples staked their claims.

In Abraham's day the city of Ur was actually on what we today would call the Persian Gulf, but massive amounts of silt have flowed down between the Rivers Euphrates and Tigris. The site of Ur is now considerably inland as a result of the silting up of the river.

Ships of the Desert in Modern Times

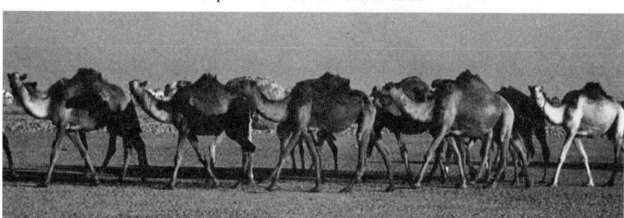

Camels, the "ships of the desert" were not commonly used in Abraham's time, but bones and figurines indicate that they were indeed utilized by some traders, such as wealthy Abraham.

Camels in the Desert

Camels are a common sight in the Middle East, and they have been so through the centuries. It is not long since critics claimed that Abraham could not have had camels, such as those which his servant took when he set out to find a bride for Isaac. However, figurines of camels have been found at Al-Ubaid, at Uruq, at Lagash, and in Egypt — some supposedly as long ago as 5,000 years. One even showed a man alongside his kneeling camels. Camel bones and teeth have been found in Palestine dating to about 1700 B.C.

The camel was not as widely used in Abraham's time as it was in the times of Solomon, but nevertheless it is now quite clear from archaeological evidence that there were indeed camels in use in the days of Abraham, just as the Bible makes clear.

There are many areas touching everyday life where the Bible is shown to be remarkably consistent and true to local conditions and circumstances. So it is with Abraham's use of camels, and references to other areas of background also — such as gods of surrounding nations, and even official titles of the enemy.

Other animals besides camels are correctly referred to — such as the first mention of the horse in the Bible, at the generally recognized time when the horse was domesticated in Egypt (Gen. 47:17).

Limestone Camel from Hebron

This limestone camel was reportedly found at Hebron in southern Palestine, dating to the times of Abraham. It was apparently a child's toy — many other toys were made out of material from the earth.

We have seen that some scholars have claimed that camels were not domesticated as early as Abraham,

Limestone Camel from Hebron

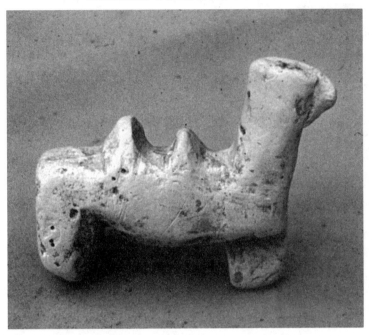

This limestone camel from Hebron supposedly dates to the time of Abraham — maybe a child's toy.

being associated with the time of Solomon. However, we also saw that the critics have been proved wrong. Actually the references to animals in the Bible are often demonstrations of the correct use of local color in the Bible records. Thus, flocks of sheep would lie down in the midst of ancient Nineveh (Zeph. 2:14), whereas shepherds would not make their fold in Babylon (Isa. 13:20). These are opposite prophecies, but each has been fulfilled accurately.

The references to camels are also accurate. Abraham's servant certainly could have had camels with him when he set out to find a bride for Isaac (Gen. 24:10). It is interesting to note that camels were used for this long journey, but on a much shorter journey when Abraham went to Jerusalem, it was by donkey (Gen. 22:3).

It is true that the camel "came into its own" in the times of Solomon, about 1,000 years after Abraham. For instance, it became important as a replacement for the slow, plodding donkey carrying spices and other trade items across desert territory. Nevertheless, the camel was sometimes used much earlier, as in the times of Abraham —just as the Bible makes clear. It has a habit of being "right after all"!

The City of Haran

Abraham's father, Terah, had taken Abraham out of their original home in Ur of the Chaldees, a leading center of moon worship, "to go into the land of Canaan." However, instead he merely traveled up the Euphrates Valley "unto Haran, and dwelt there" (Gen. 11:31). Haran was a sister city to Ur, still in the same kind of religious environment. As with Ur, the worship of the moon god was prominent.

We are further reminded of the city of Haran when we read Joshua's last charge to the people. Joshua 24:15 states:

> And if it seem evil unto you to serve the Lord, choose you this day whom you will serve; whether the gods which your fathers served that were on the other side of the flood [river], or the gods of the Amorites, in whose land you dwell: but as for me and my house, we will serve the Lord.

Haran

![Haran beehive huts]

These modern beehive huts at Haran are similar in type to others excavated in the general areas that Abraham came from. These ancient styles are still found in areas of Iraq and Syria.

Joshua's exhortation to the people was necessary: "Put away . . . the strange gods which are among you, and incline your heart unto the Lord God of Israel" (Josh. 24:23).

Another View at Haran

This challenge to serve the Lord is the same choice that can confront every normal person in every age. One can either serve the true God of creation and redemption who is now revealed in Jesus Christ, or he can serve the pagan nature gods of the world system with its evolutionary pantheism. He can, of course, unsuccessfully attempt to serve both, as it seems Abraham's father Terah and his uncle Nahor tried. However, the true God "is a jealous God" (Josh. 24:19). He will not share His glory with another.

We have already seen that the term "the flood" really is a reference to the River Euphrates. Terah, Abraham's father, and earlier ancestors apparently served the gods that were commonly worshiped in Ur and Haran, with special prominence given to Nannar the moon god.

Abraham came out from it all, and eventually left the halfway house of Haran. He moved into the land of Canaan where he would worship only the true God of Israel.

A Close-up of Beehive Huts at Haran

The clothing on the line outside these beehive huts reminds us that modern people are living here.

Beni Hasan Tomb Painting

This tomb painting dates to about 1900 B.C., and it shows Semites coming into Egypt under the protection of the Eye of Ra, seen over the head of the second man in the picture. Likewise, Abraham could have journeyed into Egypt.

Semites Visit Egypt

In the Genesis record, Abraham is shown as going down into Egypt, and it has sometimes been pointed out that this was unlikely because of the sense of resentment of the Egyptians towards various Semitic wandering people. However, this picture is from the famous Beni Hasan tombs on the Nile, and they show Semitic peoples visiting Egypt about 1900 B.C. — not long from the time of Abraham.

Notice that "the eye of Ra" can be seen at the top center of the picture (slightly to the right), demonstrating that the protection of the sun god Ra was upon these visitors. They were clothed in typical Semitic raiment, women having longer dresses than those of the men. The man at the back left is carrying a large crossbow, while the man next to him is actually carrying a harp — again reminding us that music was well-established long before the days of David with his instrument of ten strings. The donkey is carrying the bellows that were needed for the making of fire.

We could well imagine some of Abraham's people carrying the various implements that are associated with this group of Semitic people as they moved into Egypt. This picture from Beni Hasan makes it clear that Semites could come into Egypt at various times, such as is shown in the records in the Bible about Abraham.

Alalakh Tablet

Sir Leonard Woolley excavated at Atshanah, some 14 miles east of Antioch to the north of the Orontes River from 1937 to 1939, and from 1946 to 1949.

This large oval tell had some 17 occupation levels that were

Alalakh Tablets

This tablet gives a census of armed men: the first reference to Canaanites in the Alalakh tablets, dating to about the 15th century B.C., and reminding us of the reference in Genesis 14 to Abraham's 318 men. Some tablets actually listed the various ranks of such private armies. Abraham's trained servants are properly referred to as "hanikim," a word correctly used, meaning "retainers."

tentatively dated from 3100 B.C. to 1200 B.C. Tablets such as this one from Alalakh are of importance to Old Testament studies because they give new information about the history of Syria in the 18th and 15th centuries B.C. They also provide comparative material to other tablets from Mari, Nuzi, and Ugarit (the modern Ras Shamra).

They throw considerable light on the history, customs, religion, culture, and even the language close to the times of the patriarchs. Indirectly they do a great deal to throw light on the patriarchal records, such as the similarity to the story of Isaac being given a bride at the time that the servant set out to fulfil the wish of Abraham in this matter (Gen. 24).

At Alalakh the bridegroom asks a man for his daughter, to be given to him as a bride. He brought the betrothal gifts as in the Isaac story. (See also the practice when Jacob was similarly involved in a betrothal gift: Gen. 24:23 and 34:12.)

Ancient Sodom?

Excavations and surveys have taken place at a series of ancient cities. Some scholars believe these are the "Cities of the Plain" destroyed in Abraham's day.

Ancient Sodom?

This is the partially excavated site of Khanazir on the east side of the Dead Sea, and some scholars believe that this is actually the site of ancient Sodom. There are a series of wadis (streams) which flow down to the edges of the Dead Sea, and ruins of cities have been found at a number of these. The argument is that they include the Cities of the Plain referred to at the time of the destruction of Sodom and Gomorrah, in Genesis 19.

This is in opposition to the possibility that these cities were actually under the southern part of the

Dead Sea. These recently recovered ruins are along the eastern side of the southern part of the Dead Sea — on the Moabite side.

If these ARE the "Cities of the Plain," it is possible that the excavated area is front of us is actually the area of the gate at which Lot sat when he went to Sodom. He first pitched his tent towards Sodom, but eventually he was sitting in the gate. This indicated that he had become recognized as an elder of the city, one to whom people would come at the gate and put their cases before him and accept his judgment, such as in the settling of disputes.

In a *Bible and Spade* article ("Have Sodom and Gomorrah Been Found?") Dr. Bryant Wood states,

> We can say in summary that all of the evidence we have in hand at this time points to the identification of the Early Bronze sites discovered by Schaub and Rast as Sodom, Gomorrah, and the Cities of the Plain.

A Possible Reconstruction of the Destruction of Sodom and Gomorrah

Whether the "Cities of the Plain" were under what later became the southern part of the Dead Sea, or were on the sites identified by Schaub and Rast, it is very likely that God utilized natural forces to bring about the destruction. Our picture suggests the oil, gas, sulphur, salt, bitumen, etc. were due to great pressure on the submerged oil field. Marl of the various strata have been found compressed together on Jebel Usdum (Mount Sodom) on the WEST side of the Dead Sea, as by fire. Thus God rained upon Sodom and Gomorrah brimstone (and bitumenous material) and fire out of heaven, and overthrew those cities (Gen. 19:24-25). We do not rule out the miraculous activity of God in the destruction of the wicked cities. However, we also recognize that at times His miracles involved His control over the forces of nature.

Such a massive destruction could have left its impact on BOTH sides of the Dead Sea. As to the possibility of the cities being underneath the southern part of the Dead Sea, the topography of that part of the earth's surface is interesting for another reason — for at Genesis 14:2 we read of "The Valley of Siddim, which is the Salt Sea." We shall see that this is an interesting piece of local color.

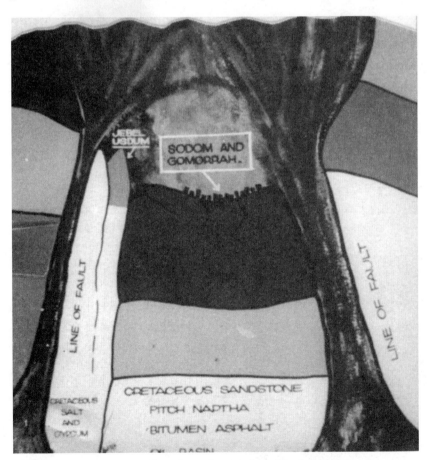

Did God use an earthquake to destroy the wicked cities of Sodom and Gomorrah? This reconstruction probably fits the facts recorded in Genesis 19.

Floating in the Dead Sea

Here is my late wife, Avis, and I, with other visitors to the Holy Land, floating in the Dead Sea. It is impossible to sink in this body of water where not even fish can live. The Dead Sea has fantastic potential chemical wealth. In his *Israel Guide*, Dr. Zev Zilmay states that the mineral deposits in the Dead Sea have been estimated to be:

22 thousand million tons of magnesium chloride,

11 thousand million tons of sodium chloride,

7 thousand million tons of calcium chloride,

2 thousand million tons of potassium chloride, and

1 thousand million tons of magnesium bromide.[24]

It is impossible to sink in the Dead Sea. No fish or other living things can survive in the Dead Sea.

The various productions from the Dead Sea are a very important item in Israel's export trade.

Dr. Zilmay makes the further point that the water contains about 25 percent of solid substance, with chloride of sodium (common salt) contributing 7 percent.

Salt at Edge of the Dead Sea

These two excavators are visiting the Dead Sea, and are examining the salt that is so plentiful along its edges. At the southern part of the Dead Sea there is a layer of salt which is said to be 150 feet deep, extending for about 15 miles. Layers of salt and sulphur are relatively close to the surface. Apparently these were caught up in the process that led to the destruction of Sodom and Gomorrah: the salt layer was ruptured along with the others, and massive quantities were hurled into the air.

A person caught in a snowstorm could be buried in snow and frozen, and it seems that Lot's wife was caught in falling salt. Possibly God used processes of nature in this miraculous happening.

The hills close to the southern end of the Dead Sea have been covered with salt, which appears to have been precipitated upon them. The story of the salt being involved in this catastrophe makes far better sense than critics would have recognized even a generation ago.

The destruction of Sodom and Gomorrah is one of the sensational Bible stories on which light has been thrown in modern times. The evidence for the veracity of the

This salt stretches for some 15 miles along the edge of the Dead Sea, and it is about 150 feet deep.

Bible writings comes from many directions. The language of the times (including obsolete words) has been retained; specific incidents have been endorsed; names and titles of surrounding peoples are often mentioned in the right context. All Bible history — including sensational stories such as the destruction of Sodom and Gomorrah — is factually recorded.

Australian Tour Leader Points to Bitumen Near the Dead Sea

Here well-known tour leader Clem Clack of Melbourne, Australia points to a heap of bitumen in the general area of Sodom. Geologists tell us that there are great deposits of salt, sulphur, and bitumen in the area. Also, the bubbles of natural gas which keep escaping point to oil deposits. Possibly such a basin was destroyed at the time of the destruction of Sodom and Gomorrah, and has now filled again.

The word translated "brimstone" actually means "bituminous material," and highly flammable bitumen is plentiful in the area. This is also referred to in the Bible in Genesis 14:10 which tells us that the Valley of Siddim was full of slime pits — pits of bitumenous material. In an early encounter (Gen. 14) the kings of Sodom and Gomorrah fell in that valley area.

Note that Siddim and Sodom are the same, utilizing the three consonants that are almost always used in Hebrew words. The vowel sounds will vary according to other words that are used.

There are many examples of the names of Bible cities and towns being retained into modern times.

Clem Clack of Melbourne, Australia, points to bitumen at the Dead Sea area. It is another way of interpreting the word "brimstone" which God used in the destruction of Sodom and Gomorrah.

Jerusalem is of course one; Beth-shan (now Beth-shean) is another; and S'dom (the ancient Sodom) is in the same category.

Salt Line in the Dead Sea

This is not a great wave, but a line of salt in the Dead Sea itself. The sea is important in many ways that a tourist would not think of until the area is visited.

At first sight this white strip in the top half of the picture looks like a gentle line of breakers in the sea, but it is actually a line of salt, not far from the site that Jewish people recognize as Sodom.

In ancient times salt was used for both secular and religious purposes — it was, for instance, one of the ingredients used in the spice that was burned when an offering was made at the temple in Jerusalem. When the Turks controlled the "Holy Land," Bedouin in the area used primitive methods to mine the salt and to sell it at the markets in Hebron and Jerusalem. Today much more sophisticated methods are used for its extraction.

Salt is not only in the sea: it is embedded in the whole face of the cliffs of Har S'dom, on the west side of the southern part of the Dead Sea. Once the factuality of the Bible story is accepted, it becomes obvious that massive quantities of salt will be distributed around this area.

And it is.

The Mountain at Masada

This is the mountain at Masada where over 900 Jews committed suicide in A.D. 72. From Masada it is possible to recognize that the southern part of the Dead Sea is again becoming uncovered.

Masada

Masada is the famous fortress where over 900 Jews perished rather than surrender to the Romans in A.D. 72. The name apparently comes from the Hebrew word Metsuda, which means "stronghold," and it was a fortress guarding the summit of this mount. Masada is the Hellenized form of the word, and it appears as such in ancient literature.

It is possible that this is the site referred to when David fled from Saul, and we read, "David and his men got them up into the stronghold [Metsuda]" (1 Sam. 24:22).

There is a further reference to the stronghold, the Metsuda, at 1 Chronicles 12:9, again telling how David's followers joined him out there in the wilderness. Apparently Masada was the meeting place.

Masada is relevant to our understanding of the topography at the time of the destruction of Sodom and Gomorrah. From the top of Masada it is plain that the northern and the southern parts of the Dead Sea are no longer one body of water. The depletion of supply from the River Jordan on both the Jordan and Israel sides (for agricultural and other purposes) means that nowhere near as much water is flowing into the northern part, and the southern part has become greatly depleted, as our diagrams have shown.

Part of the Dead
Sea Area from
Masada

*The Jordanians and
Israelis to the north
are draining much of
the Jordan River into
their own land for
agricultural purposes.
The southern Dead
Sea is reverting to its
state of centuries ago.*

The Sea Becomes Land

It is interesting to read in Genesis 14:3 that the Vale of Siddom had become the Salt Sea. That is an editing note, added by a later hand, to make it clear that the southern part of the Dead Sea was once the Valley of Sodom (variously spelt as Siddim or even as S'dom).

In the picture above we are looking across the area between the north and south portions of the Dead Sea to the mountains of Moab. These mountains, of course, are not in Israel, for the Dead Sea is part of the border between Israel and Jordan. In the foreground we see dry ground, but in fact this is actually the ground in between the northern and the southern parts of the Dead Sea. In the middle of the picture white salt can be seen, salt that is associated with the Dead Sea. Even 20 years ago this area was covered by water, and we see before us a stark reminder of the fact that the southern part of the Dead Sea is drying up because the water supply flowing in from the River Jordan has been dramatically decreased as both the Israelis and the Jordanians have siphoned off the water for their own purposes.

Another View of Dry Land in the Dead Sea Area

This photograph that I took illustrates the way in which there has been a dramatic change in this area between the northern and southern parts of the Dead Sea. I took similar photographs some ten years previously, and the

This was part of the Dead Sea only a few years ago. The Valley of Siddim (Sodom) had indeed been covered by water, but it is now reverting to the state it was in in Abraham's time.

whole area was thoroughly covered by water. If this process continues at the present rate, before long it is likely that the whole area of the southern part of the Dead Sea will again be a great valley, capable of being fertilized, even as it was in the days of Abraham. When Abraham viewed it from the mountain area where he pitched his tent and built an altar between Bethel and Ai, it was described as being well irrigated "before the Lord destroyed Sodom and Gomorrah" (Gen. 13:10).

There is an interesting verse at Ezekiel 16:55:

> When your sisters, Sodom and her daughters shall return to their former estate . . .
> then you and your daughters shall return to your former estate.

Possibly the prophet Ezekiel was looking forward to a time when it would indeed be possible to build again in the general area that was once a great valley. Perhaps coming events are casting their shadows as we see the way the waters are receding.

Canal Constructed for the Supply of Water to the Dead Sea Chemical Company

This canal was constructed so that the Dead Sea water would be available to the Dead Sea Chemical Company for panning and other purposes. The receding of the water is dramatic.

A Necessary Canal

If it were not for this canal running across that area between the northern and the southern parts of the Dead Sea, there would literally be no water between the two parts. This canal is there to supply necessary water to the Dead Sea chemical industries that are located on the western side of the southern edges of the Dead Sea.

The whole of this area is in the Great Rift Valley which extends from Mount Hermon in the north, right through into Egypt. At the Dead Sea level this rift is 1,300 feet below the level of the Mediterranean Sea, and in the northern part of the Dead Sea its bed is yet another 1,300 feet deep. It is little wonder that this rift is called the "Great Rift Valley." Alongside the Dead Sea area there are great cracks, or "faults," as they are called by geologists, and earth tremors take place there frequently.

Perhaps there will be important finds made in this former valley area if and when the waters have fully receded. The northern part is about 1,300 feet deep, but the southern part is only about 15 feet deep.

Going into "Chimney Cave"

This is the remarkable Chimney Cave, with its sides encased in rock salt. This is an ancient cave, and it is an evidence of the fact that salt was very plentiful, even back in the days of Abraham.

Entering Chimney Cave

This group of tourists is about to enter the famous Cave of the Chimney. It is a remarkable phenomenon in part of the area known as Har Sedom (which when translated means Mount Sodom) on the west side of the Dead Sea. It is not possible to be specific as to the area supposedly associated with Lot's wife, but as caves such as this are examined it is certainly clear that the Bible record fits the local topography.

Here is the sign depicting Cave of the Chimney:

> Arubotaim Cave
>
> (The Chimney)
>
> This chimney-like form was created by the action of water dissolving salts.
>
> This is an example of how caves in Sdom area were formed.
>
> Be careful to preserve this natural site.
>
> DO NOT LITTER

(It is interesting that the English half-vowel is omitted in Sdom.)

Inside the Arubotaim Cave

Here chemist Walter Pike chips away some of the rock salt in the walls of Chimney Cave. It is indeed rock salt, and the quantity of such salt almost has to be seen to be believed.

A Chemist Looks at the Rock Salt

This is chemist Walter Pike of Melbourne, Australia, peeling off some of the rock salt inside the Cave of the Chimney. It was a simple matter to peel it off with a pocket knife, for the whole wall was plastered with salt.

This mountain, with its deposits of crystalline salt, is about five miles long and some 300 feet high, stretching along the shore at the southern end of the Dead Sea, on the western side. The range is traditionally called Har Sedom (Mt. Sodom) because it has long been believed that the ancient city of Sodom was in the general vicinity.

Chimney Cave is very impressive — and beautiful — as a tourist attraction. It is also thought-provoking to think back to the happenings described in Genesis 19 when the whole area witnessed the phenomenon of fire and bitumen being rained down from the sky. If the eruption emanated from the Dead Sea itself, both eastern and western sides would have been affected. The massive quantities of salt on Har Sedom certainly suggest a dramatic upheaval.

Looking Out from the Cave of the Chimney

It is very impressive simply to be inside this cave with its rock salt all around its walls. It is just as impressive to look out to the blue sky beyond the towering mountains themselves. This whole range has vast quantities of rock salt on its face.

In such a setting one can well imagine the heaven not being blue but black as the destruction described in Genesis 19 took place in this whole area — on both sides of the Dead Sea.

Bible writers accepted the factuality of this story of the destruction of Sodom and Gomorrah: it is told factually in Genesis, then it is referred to in the Book of Deuteronomy, as well as by the prophets Amos, Isaiah, Jeremiah, Ezekiel, and Zephaniah. It is even mentioned in the Book of Lamentations.

Our Lord himself referred to the destruction a number of times as evidence that God's judgment could fall (Matt. 10:15, 11;24; Luke 10:12, 17:29).

In addition, the apostles Paul and Peter, as well as Jude, referred to it. Also, the city of sin is spiritually referred to as Sodom in the Book of Revelation.

Looking Out from "Chimney Cave"

As one looks out through Chimney Cave, it is a magnificent view. It is awe-inspiring to look up to the blue sky with a towering mountain of salt jutting into the picture.

"Lot's Wife"

This great pillar is colloquially called "Lot's wife" by some of the local people — there are other pillars likewise pointed out. We do NOT suggest that Mrs. Lot was inside any of them.

However, this is a mountain that includes a great deal of rock salt, and it is quite possible that Lot's wife was literally encased in such salt as it fell back to the earth. If people in Pompeii could be overcome by volcanic ash, it is entirely reasonable to believe that a woman fleeing from Sodom could be overcome by rock salt.

Many local people (without proof!) suggest that this or one of the other "pillars" is Lot's wife. Such pillars do show that a woman could have been encased in the falling rock salt.

Pillars containing great quantities of rock salt are plentiful in the area, and — as we have seen — salt can actually be scraped from the rocks without undue trouble.

The incident of Lot's wife was a literal happening and it also conveys an important spiritual lesson. God runs to meet the returning prodigal (Luke 15:20), and waits before judgment is executed (Gen. 6:3, 13-14, etc.) However, when His mercy is rejected, judgment falls — as it did on Lot's wife when she procrastinated beyond the time finally allowed by God.

Dead Sea Chemical Works at Sedom (Sodom)

The value of chemicals in the Dead Sea has been recognized through the centuries, but the most serious efforts to extract the wealth from this vast area was commenced only in 1930 on its northern shore. Then a second factory was erected at Sedom — as we have seen, named after the ancient Sodom. In the so-called War of Liberation in 1948, the northern plant was destroyed, but in the years that followed a new highway was extended south to Sedom. The Dead Sea Works commenced operations at the southern factory in 1952.

The Dead Sea Chemical Works

These works are tremendously important for Israel's economic welfare. Vast mineral wealth is recovered each year from the Dead Sea. Other nations are very aware of the potential.

Salt mines are in the area, but there are vast amounts of other mineral wealth, also. In fact, the wealth being recovered by the Dead Sea Chemical Works is very important for Israel's export trade. The potential is so great that Israel herself could be the subject of attack if for no other reason than to claim this unique treasure. There is no other area of the earth's surface with this type of wealth in such a confined space.

The modern State of Israel has made giant strides in the realization of its potential, but the massive project will be an effective operation for many years to come.

Professor Drori Shlomo

Professor Shlomo is one of the recognized authorities as to the great importance of the Dead Sea for Israel's export trade. His lectures are authoritative, stimulating, and of tremendous interest. He is able to give in great detail the evidence for the great importance of the southern part of the Dead Sea for Israel's economic welfare. At the same time he is also an authority in relation to the geology of the area and the general topography. He has impressive diagrams to show the way in which the volume of water in the Dead Sea has changed over the years.

The whole Dead Sea is about 40 miles long by 10 miles wide. Massive precipitation of the salt deposits in the Dead Sea has resulted from magnas and waters ascending from the depths below the earth. They are volcanic phenomena.

Various aspects of natural phenomena are a sufficient explanation to many scientists for the eruptions at Sodom and Gomorrah. Christians can accept such an explanation as a real possibility. The use of natural phenomena, divinely timed, could have been His chosen methodology.

Professor Drori Shlomo

Professor Shlomo explained about the immense wealth of the Dead Sea, its importance for Israel's economic welfare, and the geologic factors. His knowledge and insights are impressive.

Diagram of the Water Volume in the Dead Sea

The southern part of the Dead Sea is of relatively recent origin. This area is in the lowest part of the earth, being about 1,300 feet below the level of the Mediterranean. The Sea of Galilee to the north is 630 feet below the level of the Mediterranean, and the River Jordan flows from the Sea of Galilee down into the Dead Sea.

There is a dramatic absorption rate in the Dead Sea, but not sufficient over the centuries to have taken off all the water flowing in from the Jordan. The Dead Sea had no southern outlet as such, and so through many centuries there has been a gradual filling up of the area that was once the "Vale of Siddim."

In Genesis 14:3 there is a reference to the "Vale of Siddim — which is the Salt Sea." This is clearly stating that the southern part of the Dead Sea was once a valley, and it was so when the Genesis record was first committed to writing. However, the Jewish people had such respect for the written records that it would have been unusual for them to alter them. In the main, they simply added an editing note where appropriate. In this case we are told that the Vale of Siddim had become the Salt Sea.

Diagram Showing Regression of the Dead Sea

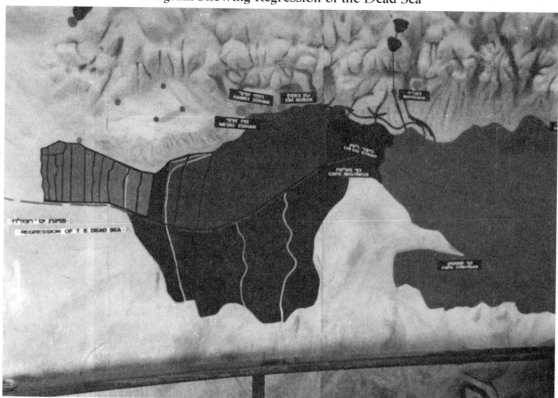

Professor Shlomo gives dramatic presentations showing how the southern part of the Dead Sea is regressing, whereas previously it was expanding southward (see Gen. 14:3).

Close-up of the Diagram of the Regression of the Dead Sea

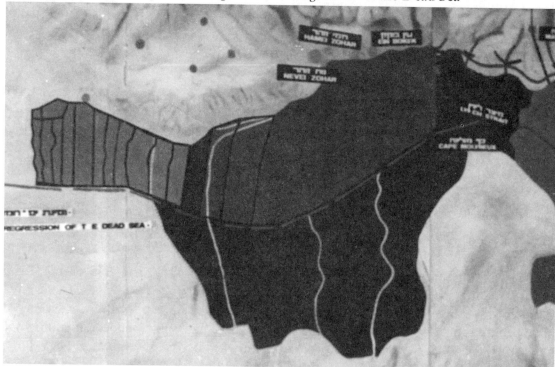

The southern part of the Dead Sea is not fully covered, as it was even 20 years ago — partly because Israel and Jordan have utilized waters from the Jordan for agricultural and other purposes.

Close-up Diagram of the Dead Sea Water Volume

The diagram at the bottom of the opposite page is a close-up of the one at the top. We have seen that the northern part of the Dead Sea is nearly 1,300 feet deep, while in the southern part it is around 15 feet deep. This southern part has been filled by the waters that have encroached from the northern section that once was the only container of the Dead Sea, stretching across where the Lisan ("the tongue"), can be plainly seen as a divider, at what is now virtually the halfway point.

We have also seen that in recent years both Jordan and Israel have been taking water from the Jordan River, north of the Dead Sea, for irrigation and other purposes. That has meant a quite dramatic reduction of the water input into the Dead Sea, and as a result the southern part is receding.

A generation ago scholars such as Professor W.F. Albright were writing to say that Sodom and Gomorrah were buried beneath the southern part of the Dead Sea. Today that view is again being put forward quite strongly by scholars such as Professor Shlomo.

The future of the area is exciting — in a number of ways. Possibly dramatic finds — whether of ancient ruins or of evidences of former agriculture — will come to light as the process of recession continues. At some points we must necessarily have an open mind as to the possibilities of future findings.

The Amazing Story of Sodom

In 1957 Walter J. Beasley (founder/president of the Australian Institute of Archaeology) wrote a booklet, *The Amazing Story of Sodom*. In it he states,

> Professor Kyle has pointed out to us that whereas early writers such as Josephus and Strabo have mentioned that the ruins of the overturned cities of the plain were still visible in their days, such evidence is not available today because the southern waters of the Dead Sea now cover this area. The fact is that we have physical proof that the waters of this sea are constantly expanding. Professor Kyle pointed out that a Roman road once crossed the southern part of the Lisan (see map). The remains of this road can be traced to the land situated on the western side of the sea. It is therefore evident that the road which once crossed the valley has become submerged since Roman times.[25]

The position since 1957 has dramatically changed because of the circumstances outlined with this series of pictures. No longer is the Dead Sea expanding but it is receding.

One Possible Reconstruction of the Destruction of Sodom and Gomorrah (Gen. 19)

This 1957 reconstruction surveys the possible destruction. Picture 8 shows that Abraham could have seen only the smoke, not the fire, because of the intervening mountain ranges.

Explanation of the 1957 Diagram, Arguing for Sodom and Gomorrah Being Beneath the Dead Sea

Diagram No. 1 is of a section of the Jordan Rift Valley showing Mount Lebanon 6,000 feet above sea level moving on to the bottom of the Dead Sea, 2,600 feet below sea level.

No. 2 shows the end section of the Dead Sea area, with the subsidence of strata along geological fault lines.

No. 3 shows (A) the Dead Sea area with the location of the cities of the plain about 2000 B.C.; and (B) the Dead Sea in the 1950s, with portion of the sea covering the cities. A Roman road can be traced to both sides of the Dead Sea.

No. 4 — by this reconstruction Bab-edh-Dra was a high place, possibly visited annually. (This can be challenged: there were indications of continuous settlement including many burials.)

No. 5 shows the upsurge of oil, gas, sulphur, salt, bitumen, etc., due to great pressure on the submerged oil field. Marl of the various strata have been found compressed together on Jebel Usdum (Mount Sodom) as by fire.

No. 6 — The Lord rained upon Sodom and Gomorrah brimstone (sulphur and bitumenous material) and fire out of heaven, and He overthrew those cities (Gen. 19:24-25).

No. 7 — Falling salt encased Lot's wife: she looked back and "became a pillar of salt" (Gen. 19:26).

No. 8 — "Abraham [at Hebron[saw the smoke of the country went up as the smoke of a furnace" (Gen. 19:28). Abraham could not have seen the FIRE because of the intervening mountain ranges. He saw the SMOKE . . . as the smoke of a FURNACE (implying intense pressure). This is a delightful piece of eyewitness recording.

NOTE: This diagram assumes that Sodom and Gomorrah were beneath the southern part of the Dead Sea. As we have seen, the other possibility being taken seriously by some scholars is that "the cities of the Plain" were actually located on the east (Jordan) side of the Dead Sea. Archaeological evidence for a line of cities makes this a possibility. This is an area where we await further light.

Jerusalem . . . Isaac and Ishmael

In our brief survey we must at least touch on Ishmael and Isaac, sons of Abraham. When it seemed (humanly speaking) that Sarah would not be able to present Abraham with a son, she urged him to have a child by her slave girl Hagar. Abraham agreed, and Ishmael was born. From a study of law codes such as that from Eshnunna (about 1900 B.C.) and that of King Hammurabi (about 1700 B.C. — both from Babylonia) it becomes clear that this was a relatively common practice, and Abraham acted against the background and in line with the customs of his time. In accordance with those customs it was Sarah, not Abraham, who made the arrangements (Gen. 16:1-3). Hagar herself appears not to have protested: her personal security became greater by law, and her offspring was also protected. Later tablets from Nuzi in the same general area (about 1500 B.C.) show that the custom was recognized over many centuries. Abraham acted according to custom: nevertheless it was outside the revealed will of God.

An Overview of "The Old City of Jerusalem

This is "the old city." Abraham came to this general area to offer Isaac, as instructed by God. When he demonstrated faith, his hand was withheld. This was a type of the sacrifice of Christ.

It also becomes clear there was an order of inheritance rights. If the man had no heir, his senior house steward inherited, with the responsibility to care for his master's wife until she died. However, if in time the man's concubine or secondary wife produced a child, that child replaced the chief steward. If later still the man's original wife produced a son he would be the heir. As we relate all this to Scripture we find that the records are clearly depicting the custom of the time. First, Eliezer of Damascus was heir to his master Abraham (Gen. 15:2-4), being replaced by Ishmael (Gen. 15:4; 16:1), and then Isaac having the rights of the first-born (Gen. 17:20, 21:12; 25:5-6). Isaac and Ishmael came together again for the burying of their father (Gen. 25:9).

It was through Isaac that God tested Abraham as to his faith, instructing him to offer "his only son" (Gen. 22:2) on Mount Moriah (the later Jerusalem). Abraham obeyed and, in a pre-vision of the sacrifice of Jesus, Isaac was offered as a model. God told Abraham to stop when it was clear that Abraham would obey — believing that God could and would raise his son from the dead (Heb. 11:19).

The Dome of the Rock

We see, first, the actual area to which Abraham traveled: the general vicinity of modern Jerusalem. Then we see a close-up of the Muslim Dome of the Rock. This dome is on the same raised area that King David purchased for the building of the temple that was actually built in the time of his son King Solomon. The dome is built over the rock on which, traditionally, Abraham was prepared to offer his son.

The Jews were dispersed around the world, commencing with the fall of Jerusalem in A.D. 70. Eventually Jerusalem came into Muslim hands, and their famous dome was built on the same platform but slightly south of the temple site. In the Koran the Arabs claim that it was their father, Ishmael, not Isaac, who was offered. To Muslims, this dome is the third most sacred spot on earth. To the Jews "their house is left to them desolate" (Matt. 23:38), with what they regard as an abomination to God on the temple platform. To the Muslims, the Dome of the Rock (and other Arab-held Middle East territories) are a reminder of the promises that Ishmael would also become a great nation (Gen. 17:20; 21:13, 18) — but it was also declared that his hand would be against every man and every man's hand would be against him (Gen. 16:12). It is a matter of conjecture as to how different the Middle East situation would be today if Abraham had not gone ahead of God's timing by having a child, Ishmael, through the slave girl Hagar. From Mt. Moriah, Abraham and Isaac returned to Beer-sheba, the place of the well that he had dug.

The Muslim "Dome of the Rock"

Muslims believe that the rock over which this dome is built was where Ishmael (not Isaac) was offered. The prophecies about both Isaac and Ishmael have been fulfilled.

The Site of Beer-sheba

Beer-sheba was where both Abraham and Isaac had dealings with local people. It was to be the
southern extremity of Israel's territory. (Dan was the northern extremity.)

The Tell at Beer-sheba (Post-Abraham)

Abraham moved around in a nomadic style, before Beer-sheba was more closely settled. In the Old Testament Beer-sheba became important, and the expression "From Dan to Beer-sheba" came to indicate what the accepted limits of Israel were. Thus we read at 1 Samuel 3:20, "And all Israel from Dan even to Beer-sheba knew that Samuel was established to be a prophet of the Lord."

There are similar expressions at such places as Judges 20:1; 2 Samuel 3:10; 17:11; 24:2; etc. Israel again controls "from Dan to Beer-sheba," but not some of the coastal areas.

Beer-sheba was important to later Israelites because it had been associated with Abraham and other patriarchs. The name actually means "the well of the seven" or "the well of the oath." It is associated with the covenant that Abraham made with Abimelech the Philistine leader, as told in Genesis 21:25-33.

In this general area Abraham denied his wife, telling the local ruler, Abimelech, that Sarah was his sister — she was, in fact, his half-sister. The Lord protected Sarah's honor, and she was restored to Abraham. At that time Abimelech recognized that Abraham was a servant of the true God and he took sheep, oxen, menservants, and womenservants, and gave them to Abraham, and restored Sarah, his wife, to him. We also read: "And Abimelech said, Behold my land is before you: dwell where it pleases you" (Gen. 20:15).

Beer-sheba from the Air

The picture from the air on the following page gives a good idea of the way in which the tell on Beer-sheba was established. On the left-hand side a water supply can be seen, and Abraham could have dug for his water in that general area.

In so-called Chalcolithic times, according to archaeological excavation, some of the caves in the Beer-sheba area were inhabited by people who raised cattle and manufactured metal tools. Pottery and stone vessels were produced, and figurines were actually carved out of ivory and bone. Even though these people lived in caves, their craftsmanship was at a high level.

Beer-sheva from the Air

The water supply on the left-hand side of the picture, is where both Abraham and Isaac (on separate occasions) may have drawn water. (Similar activities do not mean error!)

Beer-Sheba was important in a number of periods of Israel's history. In 2 Chronicles 19:4 we read: "from Beer-sheba to the hill country of Ephraim" — Ephraim having replaced Dan because Dan was now in the northern kingdom. Elijah took his famous journey to Horeb and Beer-sheba, as recorded in 1 Kings 19:3, 8. When the Jews returned from exile in Babylon, one of the cities they settled in was Beer-sheba (Neh. 11:27, 30).

Excavations have shown there was occupation through various centuries, including the Persian and Hellenistic periods. Ten Aramaic ostraca were found dating to the 4th century B.C., dealing with everyday things such as the distribution of wheat and barley.

The Well in Abraham's Day

Abraham pitched his tent in the general area of Beer-sheba and we read in Genesis 21:23-34, "And Abraham planted a grove in Beer-sheba, and called there on the name of the Lord, the everlasting God. And Abraham sojourned in the Philistines' land many days."

Abraham clearly knew the Lord, and when he "called on the name of the Lord at Beer-sheba," it was a demonstration of a vital faith. We have already commented that the most intense practical out-working of that faith was seen in his preparedness even to offer his son Isaac as he set out from Beer-sheba and went to Mount Moriah (Abraham believing that he would be resurrected by the Lord). God called to him to tell him that he was to withhold his hand. Abraham was then told by the angel of the Lord,

The Well at Beer-sheba

Although it is not possible to be definite, local tradition suggests that this well was where Abraham dug for water. As a nomad such an activity would have been necessary for Abraham.

Another View of the Well at Beer-sheba

Possibly the reason Isaac dug again at the same spot was because the wells had dried up between the time his father Abraham was there and when he himself again moved around that area.

By myself have I sworn, said the Lord, for because you have done this thing, and have not withheld your son, your only son: That in blessing I will bless you, and in multiplying I will multiply your seed as the stars of the heaven, and as the sand which is upon his enemies; and in your seed shall all the nations of the earth be blessed; because you have obeyed my voice (Gen. 22:16-18).

As Abraham and Isaac returned from Mount Moriah to Beer-sheba it is probable that Abraham shared those covenant promises with his younger son Isaac: a covenant that God later renewed with Isaac personally (Gen. 26:2-5).

In Genesis 26 we read that the servants of Isaac dug wells at a number of places, and the local Philistine people strove with them. The very fact that Isaac could dig wells that Abraham had already dug, probably indicates that they had been stopped up after a time (Gen. 26:18.)

The digging process went on, with constant tension and opposition from the local Philistines. Then we read that Isaac returned to a specific area of Beer-sheba :

And he built an altar there, and called upon the name of the Lord, and pitched his tent there: and there Isaac's servants dug a well (Gen. 26:25).

So Isaac was also associated with wells at Beer-sheba and nearby areas. The well here depicted is claimed to be that of Abraham, and that is possible. It has been a feeding place for horses, cattle, etc., from ancient to modern times.

Critics opposed the Bible record because the excavated city at Beer-sheba was later than the times of Abraham. A careful look at the Genesis record shows that Genesis is not saying there was a settled establishment there. Rather, there were wide open spaces, with men such as Abimelech able to let Abraham take land at his own choosing.

The Cave of Machpelah

This mosque is built over the cave where Abraham and some others of the patriarchal family were buried. The Genesis narrative includes a number of pointers to its integrity.

Where Sarah and Abraham Were Buried

Pictured is the Muslim mosque over the Cave of Machpelah, and in Genesis 23 we read of Abraham purchasing a cave from the sons of Heth, in which to bury Sarah. The mosque itself is not ancient, but there is good reason for scholars to accept that it is erected at the site of the ancient cave.

Earlier critics were vehement in their insistence that the Bible was wrong about this Genesis record, for they argue, the Hittites were not known as such until about the 12th century B.C. The findings at Boghazkoy (the ancient capital, Hatussas) have silenced those criticisms, for the evidence is now significant that the Hittites were indeed around in Abraham's time.

It is even true that the document referred to in Genesis 23 is like a shorthand form of a Hittite covenant treaty. There are Hittite influences within the text, such as the reference to the "full price" (verse 9 — "for as much money as it is worth"). Such casual, unobtrusive points of local color are strong evidences of eyewitness writing.

Outside the mosque under which Abraham is buried, Jewish scholar Shabtaz Herman discusses a technical point about Genesis 23 and the purchase of the cave.

A Hebrew Scholar Talks to Dr. Clifford Wilson Near the Cave of Machpelah

Here Dr. Clifford Wilson (right) and Hebrew scholar Shabtaz Herman discuss a technical point in the Hebrew Scriptures about the purchase of the Cave of Machpelah from the Hittites. The Mohammedan mosque built over the cave is in the background.

That discussion centered around the fact that there was a seemingly courteous conversation between Abraham and the wily old Hittite, Ephron, with each respecting the other and not wanting to bother about the actual ownership of the rest of the land. However, it is possible that there were, in fact, feudal dues associated with such land. If so, by his buying the whole land, Abraham would have had to pay those feudal dues. It seems that he was outwitted by Ephron at this point!

Very often we read of these points of local color, almost casually introduced into the biblical record. They consistently point to the fact that these records are the work of eyewitnesses, people who were actually there at the time. And often those same recorders of history also gave remarkable prophecies that were accurately fulfilled hundreds of years later. Their authenticity is established.

Abraham was a man of great faith. God promised to give all the land of Canaan to him and his heirs but when he died he owned only this one cave. The spiritual truth is, "He looked for a city whose builder and maker is God" (Heb. 11:10).

Abraham's Tomb in the Mosque Over the Cave of Machpelah

This sarcophagus is in the basement of the mosque. The sarcophagus itself is relatively modern but it is believed that the bones of Abraham are interred here.

Abraham's Tomb

Before us is the supposed sarcophagus (tomb) of Abraham himself in the basement of the mosque over the Cave of Machpelah. There are similar structures in this basement area for Sarah, Isaac, Jacob, and Leah.

It does seem that the actual burials — but not necessarily the containers themselves — were genuinely ancient. Scholars from the ranks of Christians, Jews, and Muslims accept that some of the patriarchs are indeed now buried in these sarcophagii.

At the time this picture was taken the mosque was protected by Jewish soldiers, with Arabs prominent in the basement area itself. Jews and Arabs regard it with considerable reverence, each people recognizing Abraham as their father. Arabs, of course, give prominence to the line of Ishmael rather than Isaac. They are descended from Ishmael.

Today the Cave of Machpelah is covered by a Middle Ages building. These sarcophagii in the basement are much later structures than the times of Abraham.

The Sarcophagus of Leah

Leah was one of the wives of Jacob, the grandson of the patriarch Abraham. The sarcophagus itself is certainly dating to a later time than that of the patriarchs, and so also is the mosque over the Cave of Machpelah. However, as stated above, Muslim, Jewish, and Christian scholars alike agree that the remains of Abraham and some of the patriarchal family are indeed interred in this area. That belief is solidly

The Tomb of Leah, Also in the Basement at Machpelah

based in history and there is good reason to believe that the remains of Leah are actually inside this receptacle.

Each of the sarcophagii in this basement area is appropriately designated as the resting place of a particular family member.

While such evidence is impressive, it is also an interesting point of contrast as we remind ourselves of a tremendously important reality concerning our Lord Jesus Christ. We cannot visit His tomb and stand alongside the remains of His body. He

Pointing to the sarcophagus that supposedly covers the bones of Jacob's wife, Leah. This area of the cave is greatly respected by both Jews and Arabs.

was crucified and buried, but on the third day He rose again. HIS tomb is empty, for He has ascended to the right hand of His Father in heaven.

Outside the Tomb of Rachel

This is the so-called tomb of Rachel, at the side of the road on the way to Bethlehem from Jerusalem.

Rachel was the mother of Jacob's son Joseph. As the first-born of his favored wife, his first choice, Joseph was special in Jacob's eyes, and he was given a distinctive coat (Gen. 37:3). This provision is somewhat similar to the distinctive statute that Hammurabi's laws allowed for the first-born of the primary wife.

This is traditionally the tomb of Rachel. (There is no archaeological evidence to support the claim.) Jewish people come here to pray and talk about Rachel.

Rachel died giving birth to Benjamin:

> So Rachel died and was buried on the way to Ephrath [that is, Bethlehem]. Over her
> tomb Jacob set up a pillar, and to this day that pillar marks Rachel's tomb (Gen. 35:19).

The identification of this site is not accepted with the same certainty as the tomb of the patriarchs at the Cave of Machpelah. Nevertheless, it is an interesting site, and possibly Rachel was buried near here, though the building itself is much later. Orthodox Jews come here quite often, referring to "our mother Rachel" in addresses given at this meeting-place inside the building.

Inside the Tomb of Rachel

Jewish scholar Shabtaz Herman is delivering an address on the virtues of Rachel, "the mother of us all." (Strictly, she was the mother only of the descendants of Joseph and Benjamin.)

At the left of our picture is Jewish scholar Shabtaz Herman giving an address, extolling the virtues of "Rachel our mother." Another Jewish adherent is seated in front of the so-called tomb of Rachel as he prays to Yahweh (Jehovah).

The gentleman giving the address is a leader of a group which is actively involved in the preparation of vestments and other objects in readiness for the re-establishment of the Jewish temple. They believe that such a happening will take place very soon.

We saw that Rachel stole her father's clay gods. But the story did not end there. When Laban caught up with them, Jacob said the death penalty would be invoked against anyone found with Laban's gods. Archaeology shows that stealing of clay gods was indeed a capital offense — but Rachel did not die at that time: if she had, this would not be her traditional tomb.

Rachel avoided her father's anger when he chased after them — she temporarily hid the stolen gods inside a camel's saddle and sat on it (Gen. 31:34-35). Later, Jacob ordered that all the clay gods of his company should be buried at Shechem: "Get rid of all the strange gods you have with you . . . we are going to Bethel" (Gen. 35:2-3). Bethel means "House of God." There could be no idolatry associated with that place! The historical background and the spiritual teachings are both important in this biblical record.

Tablets from Boghazkoy

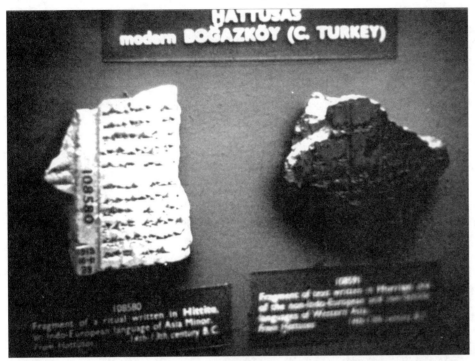

Modern Boghazkoy is the ancient Hatussas, the Hittite capital. These tablets show that Hittites were around earlier than critics claimed. Genesis 23 shows Abraham dealing with Hittites.

Hittite Documents

Even before Abraham's time, "the families of the Canaanites spread abroad" (Gen. 10:18), and some of the Hittites spread north into Anatolia. They established the great Hittite empire in what is now modern Turkey.

These tablets come from ancient Hattusas, the capital of the Hittite empire. The modern name is Boghazkoy, in central Turkey. Important documents were found there, dating to approximately the 16th century B.C., written in Hittite cuneiform. *The Epic of Gilga-*

mesh, various myths and historical texts, a law code, and a peace treaty were included in the recovered documents.

These tablets threw important light on the Hittites relatively close to the times of the patriarchs. They also demonstrated that the legal covenant forms in the writings of Moses followed the same pattern of legal forms which the Hittites used.

Important light has been thrown on the Hittite covenant documents by Professor George Mendenhall. Basically, he pointed to the fact that they showed that the covenant documents written by Moses must come from one source, and not from a whole series of strands, as required by the higher critical Documentary Hypothesis.

This HITTITE LAW CODE is one of the earliest yet found. As well as showing that the Hittites were indeed around in Abraham's time, their law code has interesting comparisons with the code of Moses, especially when Moses dealt with everyday things.

Hittite Law Code

Professor George Mendenhall's researches showed that the covenant documents within the Pentateuch not only came from one source, but also that the source itself dated to the middle of the 2nd millennium B.C. That is a dramatic pointer to the genuineness of the great man Moses having written those Pentateuch documents somewhere about 1500 B.C.

We accept the date of the Exodus as 1447 B.C. approximately, with Moses writing the law codes during the wilderness journey in the next 40 years. That is what the Bible states, and it fits the background of the times as recovered by archaeological research.

Before us is a Hittite law code from Boghazkoy (the old Hattusas) — the ancient Hittite center. It effectively answered critical arguments that Moses could not have compiled the "advanced" law code that is presented in the Pentateuch. The Hittite documents — and especially this law code — are a clear rejection of the higher critical Documentary Hypothesis which opposed the Mosaic writing of the Pentateuch.

Clay God from Mesopotamia

As well as being worshiped, such clay gods had an association with title deeds. When Rachel stole her father's clay gods, she stated there was no inheritance left for her in her father's house.

Stealing Clay Gods

In the Bible record we read of Rachel stealing her father's clay gods, and they would have looked something like this teraphim (god) from ancient Babylonia. There is good reason to believe that the clay gods were also associated with title deeds as well as being part of idol worship.

The time came when Jacob's wife Rachel was not satisfied with the way her father had treated her, and so she was very ready to listen to Jacob when he said that he was about to leave his father-in-law, Laban. With her sister Leah she said to Jacob, "Is there yet any portion or inheritance for us in our father's house? Are we not counted of him as strangers? For he has sold us, and has also quite devoured our money" (Gen. 31:14-15).

We go on in the story and read that while Laban was away shearing his sheep, Rachel went into his tent and stole his images (his gods — verse 19). Rachel believed that her inheritance had been taken from her and so she took the law into her own hands as she stole her father's clay gods.

A Nuzi Tablet

Various customs in the patriarchal records have light thrown on them from tablets found at various places — Ur, Eshnunna, Kish, Mari, Boghazkoy, Nuzi, and other sites. This one is from Nuzi — an adoption tablet later than Jacob's time but having similarities to patriarchal customs recorded at other sites dating to Abraham's time. The more they are studied, the more it is recognized that the customs recorded in the patriarchal records are authentic.

Nuzi tablets were somewhat later than Abraham's time, but they demonstrate that Bible records were eyewitness accounts, with similar customs to those of their neighbors.

Law No. 25 of the Eshnunna Law Code (about 1900 B.C.) talks about a man going into servitude so that he can have his new master's daughter as a bride. (See Ancient Near Eastern Texts.[26]) The similarity to Jacob serving Laban for Rachel and Leah is obvious (Gen. 29:18, 21). Jacob acted according to the practices in his background. Each of his two wives presented him with a handmaid by whom he had children (Gen. 25:5-6; 30:3-21).

That is similar to Laws No. 144 and 146 of the Code of Hammurabi (about 1700 B.C.), where the first wife gives a slave to her husband and he has children by her. Law No. 170 says that all the children would share the inheritance equally if their father had acknowledged them — with one proviso that "the first-born, the son of the first wife, receive a preferential share." (See the preferential treatment for Isaac at Gen. 25:5-6.)

Rachel Weeping for Her Children

In Matthew's Gospel, the application of Rachel weeping for her children is applied to the time of the birth of the Lord Jesus Christ. The wicked Herod had been told that the Messiah would be born in Bethlehem, and in an attempt to destroy the Messiah he had large numbers of Jewish children killed. Matthew relates this to the fact that these would include descendants of Rachel, and so "Rachel weeps for her children."

This statue is outside the Yad Ve'Shem memorial in Israel. It reminds us of the dreadful experiences of the holocaust during World War II, when millions of Jews lost their lives.

Matthew consistently related Old Testament incidents and prophecies to the life of the Lord Jesus Christ, often using the expression, "That it might be fulfilled."

In modern times this incident of Rachel weeping for her children has been applied by the Jewish people to the dreadful destruction of their relatives at the time of the attempt by Hitler and his Nazi subordinates to destroy the Jews in World War II. That attempt to annihilate a whole nation is now seen as one of the most dastardly activities of all human history.

John Ankerberg and His Family at the Yad Ve'Shem Memorial in Jerusalem

These stones are a reminder of the atrocities that were committed against the Jewish people.

The Yad Ve'Shem Memorial in Jerusalem is in an impressive area of buildings and statues. The Warsaw uprising is depicted in stone, and also the fact that millions died in Nazi Germany, Austria, and other centers during World War II.

Sadly for the Jewish people, they were dispersed abroad after the Fall of Jerusalem in A.D. 70 (with a final stand at Masada in A.D. 73), and they were indeed dispersed to the four corners of the earth.

The holocaust, whereby some six million Jews are said to have been annihilated, was dreadful. To some extent it is seen by many Bible students as a prophetic fulfilment of prophecies about a people who as a race, then and now, rejected their Messiah.

It is a sobering thought that there are far more Arab descendants of Ishmael in the world today than there are Jews. Their hatred for the Jews is well-documented as is the attempted pogrom by Hitler and his hordes.

John Ankerberg at the Yad Ve'Shem Memorial

המדינה לומאה ותמישים ריבוא ילדי ישראל שנסמו בשואה
חזם בתרומתם של אברהם ואדירה שפיגל מבוורלי הילם, קליפורניה,
לזכר בנם עזראל הילד, שנספה באושוורץ בשנת תש"ד.

MEMORIAL TO THE ONE AND A HALF MILLION JEWISH CHILDREN WHO PERISHED IN THE HOLOCAUST,
ERECTED THROUGH THE GENEROSITY OF ABRAHAM AND EDITA SPIEGEL OF BEVERLY HILLS, CALIFORNIA,
IN MEMORY OF THEIR SON UZIEL, KILLED IN AUSCHWITZ IN 1944.

*John Ankerberg hosts the "John Ankerberg Show," dealing largely with biblical evidences. Here he is outside the
memorial to the millions who lost their lives in that dreadful holocaust.*

John Ankerberg is the host of the "John Ankerberg Show," which goes out over a large network of
television stations in the United States. They major on apologetics, the defense of Scripture, and insistence
on the rightness of the Christian faith.

John Ankerberg is co-author of *The Case for Jesus the Messiah*. Among other things he makes it clear
that Old Testament prophets declared that the Jewish people would return to their land, and that the return
that has taken place in this 20th century demonstrates that the times of the end are near. Jewish people are
returning in large numbers from the ends of the earth to Israel, their Promised Land.[27]

However, those same prophets also declared that Israel would be dispersed among the nations — and
they have been, for nearly 2,000 years since the time of Christ on earth. And the prophets declared that
they would know dreadful persecution — and that, too, has come to pass, especially in the Nazi holocaust
of World War II.

The Yad Ve'Shem Memorial in Jerusalem is a permanent reminder of those millions whose lives
were taken at that time, for no other reason than that they were Jewish.

Remembering the Children at Yad Ve'Shem

An impressive display reminds the visitor that vast numbers of innocent children were also destroyed at the time of the oppression of the Jews by Hitler and his Nazi followers.

Memorial to the Children Annihilated in the Holocaust

One of the most impressive aspects of the Yad Ve'Shem memorial is in a building telling of the way children were destroyed. This area of stones outside is also a memorial to that dreadful happening.

Inside the building there are electric lights to convey the impression of the gradual extinguishing of these young lives. As one goes through the guiding rails in the near-darkness, the names of children are read out in a mournful style which is most depressing. Vast numbers of children died in the gas chambers of Germany, Austria, and elsewhere — again, for no other reason that that they were Jewish. This was one of the greatest crimes of all history.

Jesus used a child as an example of how men should be as children in their reactions, and He taught that kindness to children would bring rewards (Matt. 10:42; 18:2-4). He urged the disciples to let the little children come to Him (Mark 10:14).

His attitude and His love were diametrically different from the hatred shown by vast numbers towards children of His own chosen race.

A Brief Summary of Section III

Section III covered the historical records in the chapters following Genesis 11. A generation ago, critical scholarship rejected Abraham as merely the personification of a tribe, and the records themselves as legends. Here are a few relevant notes on which archaeology has thrown light:

1. The remarkable finds at Ur of the Chaldees demonstrated that people died for a better resurrection;

there were 13-stringed lyres long before David; heavy gold rings, (see Gen. 24:22); trade extended far and wide; there was advanced technology, including well-preserved iron chariot rings; Ur had a huge ziggurat (temple tower), dedicated to the moon-god Nannar (see Josh. 24:15); Ur was a center of surprising knowledge and schooling (e.g. trading records, cube root, geometry, a school-house).

2. From Ur, Abraham traveled to Haran in the north. Ebla tablets refer to Haran "in the territory of Ur" — thus this was a different Ur. See Genesis 11:34 and Acts 7:3-4 — Abraham's move was from one LAND to another, not merely from one town to another nearby center.

3. A form of the name Abraham (not the same person) is known at several ancient centers such as Mari, Ur, and Ebla. It was a relatively common name.

4. Nuzi tablets (15th century B.C.) combine with other records to throw light on:

A barren wife arranging for a slave to bear a child for her (Hagar given to Abraham by Sarah, Gen. 16:1-2); a subsidiary wife and her child could not be sent away (Gen. 16:6 and 21:10-11); inheritance rights — a chief steward (Eliezer) would be replaced by a "natural" son (Ishmael), and in turn replaced by the son of the original wife (Isaac). Finding a bride for Isaac — camels, golden jewelry, marriage arrangements for a free woman, and "brothership money" are all properly referred to. There are parallels to the story, as with Shamshi I of Assyria sending to the King of Qatna in Syria to find a bride for his son.

5. Abraham lived according to established law. This is illustrated by his dealings with Hagar and Ishmael — Hagar was apparently given her freedom, not sold again; and Ishmael did not have equal inheritance with Isaac (the Lipit-Ishtar code).

6. Other tablets also are relevant, from Ur, Boghazkoi, Kish, Mari, and Ebla.

7. Ur and Haran were both centers of moon worship, involving: degradation of women; Sodomites and others served as such in worship (Rom. 1:24-32).

8. Abraham's use of camels is NOT an anachronism: figurines have been found at Al-Ubaid, Uruq, Lagash, and in Egypt; camel bones and teeth have been found in Palestine dating to about 1700 B.C.

9. The Battle of Four Kings against Five (Gen. 14): the names fit their nationalities. Despite earlier criticisms, archaeologists have found evidences of civilizations in the area; "The Valley of Siddim, that is, the Salt Sea" (Gen. 14:3) includes an appropriate editing note, for the valley area now is covered by the encroaching sea; Abraham's "hanikim" (trained servants Gen. 14:14) — this word later became obsolete, but was then in use: a pointer to "local color;" Abraham's 318 hanikim: recovered tablets from Ur tell of private armies, between 100 and 600 men.

10. The destruction of Sodom and Gomorrah (Gen. 19): these cities are possibly referred to in the Ebla Tablets (so claimed by Professor Pettinato); . . . and there are other points of confirmation.

SECTION IV

JOSEPH IN EGYPT

A GREAT MAN WHO HONORED HIS GOD

Pharaoh Sesostris III

This is possibly the pharaoh who appointed Joseph to high office in Egypt.

Joseph at Dothan

Joseph was the favorite son of his father (Gen. 37:3) and he made him the famous "coat of many colors" (or, having wide sleeves — either way, it was a coat of distinction). Joseph's brothers hated him because of their father's favoritism.

In that chapter, Genesis 37, we read of Joseph's dreams whereby the sheaves of his brothers bowed down before him. In another dream the sun and the moon and eleven stars acted in a similar way. When he

The Tell at Dothan

In obedience to his father, Joseph set out to find his brothers and to give them food. He found them at Dothan. They conspired to destroy him, then to sell him as a slave.

Dothan and the Well Outside the Tell

Joseph's brothers received him poorly, and put him in a pit. Later he was sold to passing Midianite traders. The well on the left is traditionally associated with his ordeal.

told his father Jacob and his brethren, he was rebuked, and his brothers were jealous against him.

Some time later Jacob sent Joseph to bring food to his brothers, and he set out to find them. Eventually he did so at Dothan, and the mound of Dothan is pictured here. Even before he arrived his brothers muttered against him. They determined to dispose of him, but instead they sold him to passing Midianite traders who were on their way to Egypt.

It has been argued that one record of this incident refers to Midianites, whereas another talks about Ishmaelites, thus supposedly constituting a Bible error. However, there is no contradiction, for the Midianites were simply a division of the Ishmaelites — the descendants of Ishmael (Gen. 37:25, 28).

A Well Outside Dothan

Joseph was put in a well outside the city of Dothan, and traditionally the well at the bottom left of this picture is the one referred to.

A study of the life of Joseph shows many similarities to the life of our Lord. Both were "special" in a father's eyes; both willingly came to their brethren, to provide for their need. Both were rejected by those brethren, and were treated as though they were hated enemies.

Each was sold at the current price of an average able-bodied slave (20 and 30 pieces of silver respectively), both went into "captivity," both were faithful to God in their daily activities, both have been acknowledged by at least some of their brethren, each returned good for evil in the forgiveness of his erring brethren, each was greatly exalted, each resisted temptation, each consistently honored God.

The life of Joseph is remarkable in the ways it points to that one of whom His Heavenly Father declared, "This is My beloved Son, in whom I am well pleased — hear Him!" (Matt. 17:5).

Breadmaking in Ancient Egypt

This picture from ancient Egypt shows the process of breadmaking. The finished product was carried on the head of the baker — an interesting reminder of the story in the Bible about Joseph. As told to Joseph in a dream,

This reminds us of the story of Joseph and the baker with the loaves on his head. Joseph correctly interpreted the baker's dream — he was about to be hanged, because he offended the pharaoh.

the pharaoh's baker had the bread on his head, and then it was picked from his head by the birds:

> I had three white baskets on my head; And in the uppermost basket there was all manner of bakemeats for Pharaoh: and the birds ate them out of the basket on my head (Gen. 40:16-17).

Joseph interpreted the baker's dream as meaning that he (the baker) was to lose his head. Joseph's interpretation proved to be correct, and for that he gave honor to God.

That was typical with Joseph — as can again be seen with the title referred to at Genesis 41:43 where he was made Father to Pharaoh, Lord of Pharaoh's House, and Ruler of all Egypt. The actual Egyptian title was "Father to the Gods," but Joseph could not regard the Pharaoh as God, so he Hebraized it and made it "Father to the Pharaoh."

The three titles are known, and they indicate respectively that Joseph was chief counselor to the pharaoh, he was in charge of palace affairs, and he was the chief official for all of Egypt — Joseph had responsibility in regard to pharaoh's person, his palace, and his provinces.)

The Chief Baker — and Other Titles

Acknowledgment of receipt of wheat by the chief baker of the Temple of Amun from the temple bailiffs.

Critics claimed that Old Testament titles in the story of Joseph were used incorrectly. But this title is a reminder that the Bible writers knew of local customs and titles.

A number of titles are correctly recorded in the Joseph story in Genesis. Thus we read that Joseph was made the "merper" (overseer) in Potiphar's house (Gen. 39:4-5). There are other titles in Genesis 40:2–3: the captain of the guard, the chief of the butlers, and the chief baker (despite claims that the title was unknown, it was authentic, as shown in this inscription.)

Even the word "pharaoh" was a title, meaning "the great house" — it later came to mean "king." This was actually an early way of designating the ruler, whereas at later times it was more usual to add the pharaoh's name. That also is seen in the Bible, as with Pharaoh Sheshonk (1 Kings 11:40); Tirhakah (2 Kings 19:9, Isa. 37:9); Hophra (Jer. 43:30); and Necho (Jer. 46:2). The Bible writers were contemporary with the events they described.

The same principle is found at other places, such as with the use of the word "Tartan" at Isaiah 20:1, meaning a commander of the Assyrian army. The Bible writers correctly used the titles of the people with whom they were in contact, and this is a real indication of the authenticity of the records. Other peoples' titles would not usually be used by the Hebrews except where there was contact with the "foreign" peoples themselves.

Seven Cows in Egypt

Hathor, the cow goddess of Egypt, is followed by the sacred bull, Apis. Sometimes (not always) seven cows depicted seven regions of Egypt. When the pharaoh saw seven cows it was probably this symbolism that God used to convey truth through Joseph.

Hathor, the Cow Goddess

The interpretation of dreams was very important in Egypt. In the Joseph story we have already referred to Joseph's dreams before he came to Egypt, and then in Egypt he correctly interpreted the dreams of both the butler and the baker. Later, he correctly interpreted the pharaoh's dreams also.

One of the dreams of the pharaoh included two groups of seven cows. The seven cows possibly spoke of Hathor, the cow goddess of love, who ruled over the seven regions of Egypt (the number of regions varied at times). ALL Egypt — ALL seven regions — would be dramatically affected by the famine.

In this picture Hathor is shown as seven cows, followed by the sacred bull Apis.

The fact that the dream was repeated in another form (with wheat) meant that it was to happen very soon, and Joseph urged that action should be taken forthwith (Gen. 41:14-36).

A Pharaoh with the Ears of a Cow

A Pharaoh Shown with the Ears of a Cow

Notice that this pharaoh's ears are the ears of a cow, in honor of the cow god, Hathor. She was a prominent deity amongst the many deities of Egypt.

We often find in Scripture that the background of

Egyptian pharaohs were supposed to be the manifestation of various gods, including Hathor, the cow goddess of love, as seen in statue. Vast numbers of "deities" were honored in Egypt.

the times is used to illustrate or elaborate divine truth. These become pointers to the authenticity of the record as truth continues to "spring out of the earth" (Ps. 85:11).

The priests would have had to acknowledge the wisdom of what Joseph said, for when the interpretation about the cows was declared before them by Joseph, its correctness would have been obvious in their eyes, even though they had not been able to interpret it before Joseph declared its meaning. As Joseph himself said, "It is not in me: God shall give Pharaoh an answer of peace" (Gen. 41:16).

Joseph consistently gave honor to the true God Whom he served.

Seti I Rewards a High Official

Pharaoh Seti I giving a special collar of office to a high official. The happening is remarkably like that when Joseph of an earlier time was installed as the chief official in the land.

Installing a Senior Officer

This is a picture of an Egyptian vizier being installed at the time of Pharaoh Seti I, some time later than Joseph. However, it has remarkable similarities to the story we find of Joseph where he was given a gold chain of office, was arrayed in gold linen, given the pharaoh's seal, and recognized as second only to the pharaoh in authority.

Over and over again we find that the local color of the Egyptian activities is remarkably accurate. At one stage we read of one of Joseph's titles being merper (overseer) — the word is now known from archaeology. Zaphnath-Paaneah was a new name or title also given to Joseph by the pharaoh, and it also is now known from archaeology. It has the idea of "Head of the Sacred College — one who reveals secrets."

The Sed Festival was an important occasion when the chief of the priests was honored in a special way as a representative of the gods. (The pharaoh himself was supposedly Ra the sun god incarnate.) Joseph was indeed greatly honored when he was given the name Zaphnath-Paaneah — to the chagrin of the priests!

Joseph Was Given the Pharaoh's Seal

Joseph was given the pharaoh's signet seal, and this indicated that he was to have the authority of the pharaoh. None dare oppose him, at the risk of their lives. The record of Joseph's installation as the vizier, the prime minister of the land, is remarkably similar to that which is known in other records from Egypt.

This is what we read at Genesis 41:42:

> And Pharaoh took off his ring from his hand, and put it upon Joseph's hand, and arrayed him in vestures of fine linen, and put a gold chain about his neck.

The gold signet ring here pictured is from the tomb of the young Pharaoh Tut-Ankh-Amon. Such a ring would have been given to Joseph, together with a gold necklace-type chain to be worn around the neck. In Genesis 45:8 Joseph further tells his brothers of the titles pharaoh had conferred on him (as discussed above).

Signet Ring Belonging to Tut-Ankh-Amon

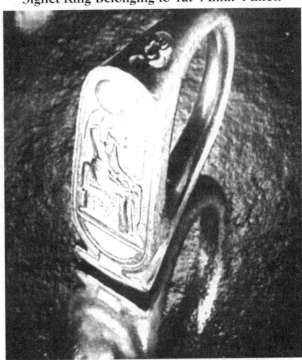

Joseph's signet ring from the pharaoh would have been somewhat like this one from the tomb of the young King Tut-Ankh-Amon. Joseph could exercise authority in the name of the pharaoh.

The Royal Chariot

Joseph was also given the pharaoh's second chariot in which to ride. It is possible that this was the time when the horse was widely domesticated in Egypt.

It is an interesting fact that there is no mention of the horse in the Bible until we read of the Egyptian people even selling their horses to buy corn from Joseph (Gen. 47:17). It would seem that this first use of the word for horse in Genesis is another indication of the local color of the Bible record. To a limited extent the horse was previously known and used — referred to as "the wild ass of the East," but it was brought into special significance in Egypt.

As Joseph drove through the land in a modified "civilian" version of such a chariot, the local people were expected to bow the knee before him, for his authority was second only to that of the pharaoh. Probably his main title was that of vizier, chief ruler of the land. However, we have already seen that he was given other titles as well (Gen. 45:8). Earlier his title under Potiphar was "overseer" (merper) of the house — another known title. Potiphar's own title, "Captain of the Guard," is also correctly used (Gen. 45:1, 4).

The local color of the Joseph story is consistently accurate, and points to eyewitness recording.

The Egyptians Were Proud of Their Light Chariots of War

Joseph was given the pharaoh's second chariot. There is reason to believe this was when the light chariot of war was introduced into Egypt.

Chariot from Tut-Ankh-Amon's Tomb

This tomb painting is from the treasures buried with the youth-king, the Pharaoh Tut-Ankh-Amon. The wealth of such a youth is almost incredible, for he was relatively insignificant.

For such wealth to be actually buried there needs to be an explanation, and it is that no matter how young or unimportant the pharaoh might be, he was still accepted as a manifestation of the sun-god. As such he must be accorded the honors due to the gods. Such wealth again highlights the credibility of the biblical reports of gold and so much more with Solomon and others.

Notice the similarity in these different chariots. Possibly one artist had access to the earlier one. Joseph would have driven up and down Egypt in such a chariot.

Joseph must have been a man of outstanding ability to become the pharaoh's senior officer. It is interesting to conjecture as to how much his commitment to Jehovah was relevant. Pharaoh was acknowledged as the physical manifestation of the sun god, yet he accepted Joseph's explanation that it was Jehovah alone who could cause the pharaoh's dream to be understood (Gen. 41:16) and that God was about to act (Gen 41:25).

Clearly Joseph claimed the superiority of Jehovah to the pharaoh. Pharaoh acknowledged Joseph, even to the high point of giving him his prized second chariot.

In passing, notice the similarity between the horses in the two pictures. They are not the same, nor from the same time. It seems possible that the man who painted the scene found with Tut-Ankh-Amon had access to the earlier one above, depicting Thutmose III who lived about the time of the Exodus (accepting the "early" date of about 1447 B.C.)

Gathering Wheat in Egypt

Joseph was given the responsibility of storing wheat in the seven years of plenty so that there would be enough in the following seven years of dreadful famine.

A late inscription dating to about 200 B.C. looks back to a time well before Joseph to describe a seven-year famine, in the days of Pharaoh Zozer who ruled in the Third Dynasty of Egypt (usually given as about 2700 B.C.) It partly states,

> I was in distress on the Great Throne, and those who are in the palace were in heart's affliction from a very great evil, since the Nile had not come in my time for a space of seven years. Grain was scant, fruits were dried up and everything which they eat was short. Every man [robbed] his companion. . . . The temples were shut up. . . . Every [thing] was found empty.[28]

Gathering the Wheat Harvest

In ancient Egypt the gathering of the harvest was tremendously important. Once again the Joseph story fits the Egyptian background.

The text goes on to tell of Pharaoh Zozer's offering to the god Khnum "in recompense for these things which thou wilt do for me."

This was NOT the seven-year famine of Joseph's day, and there are other records of droughts that extended for years. Joseph's storing of wheat clearly fitted the pattern of ancient Egyptian life.

Recording the Wheat Harvest

The wheat had to be properly recorded, and it is implicit in the story. Eventually the people had to come and buy from Joseph, who had wisely stored grain during the seven plentiful years.

Recording the Wheat Harvest

This Egyptian tomb painting shows how the grain was recorded, being gathered in great heaps before being put into the granaries. It reminds us of the authority given to Joseph as he was to go throughout the land, establishing granaries and then having a proper record of the grain which eventually would be sold to the Egyptians — and others — in their need.

Earlier we referred to an inscription ascribed to Pharaoh Zozer, telling of granaries being utilized, and of people "borrowing" from such repositories because of starvation.

The chariot at the left of the picture reminds us that Joseph also was given a chariot as the pharaoh's senior official. He, too, was able to save the people from starvation, having full authority from the pharaoh. This is what we read at Genesis 41:56–57:

And the famine was over all the face of the earth: And Joseph opened all the store-houses, and sold to the Egyptians; and the famine waxed sore in the land of Egypt. "And all countries came into Egypt to Joseph to buy corn; because the famine was so sore in all lands."

These granaries were built in the general area of the Ramesseum near the Valley of the Kings out from Thebes. Local Egyptian historians suggest they were built in the time of Joseph.

Granaries in the Valley of the Kings

These storehouses in the center of the picture are in the general area of the Ramesseum that is associated with the name of Ramses the Great of Egypt. Notice that the granaries are at a lower level than the Ramesseum, and this means they were constructed considerably earlier than the later great structures.

Local authorities from Karnak (as told to me personally) stated that they know of no ancient ruler or high official with whom these granaries could be associated other than Joseph. They recognized that he was at one time a high official in their country.

For an Egyptian authority to make such a concession is itself a strong indication that it would indeed have been Joseph, for right through the ages it has not been usual to give credit to the Israelites for whom the Egyptians have traditionally had a deep and lasting animosity.

A Closer Look at the Granaries

The Ramesseum and the granaries are in the general area of the Valley of the Kings and the Valley of the Queens near Luxor. It is not widely known that there was also "the city of the workmen." Thousands of Egyptian workmen lived in small huts, all crowded together.

Egyptian pharaohs had access to vast numbers of workmen in virtual slave conditions. With the authority vested in Joseph he would have been able to build granaries like these right through the land. One of his titles was "Ruler of all Egypt" — "Mizraim" (Egypt) being a plural form that embraced both north and south Egypt. His authority was very widespread.

Egyptian wall paintings depict great storehouses for wheat, and the Genesis stories about Egypt — famine and all — breathe the atmosphere of the times. Egypt did have famines that lasted for years, and storehouses were full so that wheat was stored against drought conditions.

An important difference in the time of Joseph was that a future time frame was given, both as to the time of prosperity and of the later famines.

Close-up of Egyptian Granaries

For Egyptian authorities to acknowledge that Joseph probably built these granaries is remarkable. They are lower level than the structures of Raamses II. They were built at an earlier time.

Israelites in Egypt

Even before the arrival of Joseph's father, Jacob, Joseph had selected Goshen as the most suitable location. This quite fertile land was at that time virtually unsettled by the Egyptians. The pharaoh himself knew that Joseph's family was coming (Gen. 45:17-20), but evidently he had not made a formal commitment as to an actual geographical location.

Joseph's influence was such that he personally could largely make the decision himself. Nevertheless, a large area of land was involved, and obviously the pharaoh's approval would ultimately be required. So it was that Joseph took five of his brothers, presented them to the pharaoh, and formally asked for land to be made available. Pharaoh responded favorably:

> And Pharaoh spake to Joseph, saying, Your father and your brethren are come unto you: The land of Egypt is before you; in the best of the land make your father and brethren to dwell; in the land of Goshen let them dwell (Gen. 45:5-6).

Joseph's Family Settled in Egypt

*This is in the Delta region of Egypt, away from the main administrative center at
Memphis. Joseph chose some of the lush areas in the land of Goshen.*

Another View of the General Area Where the Hebrews Settled

*No doubt the pharaoh greatly appreciated the efficiency and integrity of Joseph, and he willingly
agreed to let Joseph's family settle in the land of Goshen, offering work to some of the family.*

A Choice Part of Egypt

Joseph knew full well that the land of Goshen (believed to be in the Delta region of Egypt) was one of the choicest areas of ancient Egypt. He also was wise enough to recognize that the cattle-keeping Egyptians despised both sheep and shepherds. So Joseph's choosing the relatively obscure area of Goshen helped to ensure a minimum of friction with the native Egyptians. The Israelites were largely segregated.

In his wisdom Joseph instructed his brothers to emphasize that they were cattlemen rather than despised shepherds. Some scholars believe that Joseph was actually testing his brothers' honesty. The pharaoh then offered employment to some of the good workers among the Hebrews — "make them rulers over my cattle" (Gen. 47:6). Although they declared their interest as shepherds (Gen. 47:3-4), apparently the fact of having cattle was also in the conversation — with the pharaoh making his offer to employ some of them.

The region approved by the pharaoh seems to have been bordered on the west by the River Nile, for the Israelites "did eat fish freely in Egypt" (Num. 11:5). According to Psalm 78:12, their property must have included "the field of Zoan," which was on one of the outlet channels of the Nile, relatively near the sea. In general, it was close to Egypt's north-east corner. The Egyptian population tended to concentrate more to the south and west.

Joseph Changes the Title to "Father to the Pharaoh"

This modern picture of ancient Egyptian life highlights the importance of the man-god. He would be buried in a tomb on the west side of the Nile, rejoining the setting sun on its daily journey across the sky.

Joseph really tested his brothers, not knowing whether that earlier jealousy and hatred still persisted. There was the incident of the money that Joseph put into their sacks, challenging their honesty (Gen. 43), and then Joseph's own silver cup was put into Benjamin's sack.

The men feared that Joseph intended to make them slaves (Gen. 43:18), but Joseph had every intention of having a full restitution of brotherly ties, after he was satisfied as to their own character.

Joseph arranged for a private meal with his brothers. He sat apart from them in the normal Egyptian fashion (Gen. 43:32) and they all enjoyed a meal. The brothers wondered how Joesph was able to set their places in order of their age! (Gen. 43:33).

After some time Joseph revealed himself to his brothers. He told them not to be conerned "for God did send me before you, to preserve life" (Gen. 45:5).

He told about the years of plenty and then the years of famine (as revealed through the pharaoh's dreams). Then Joseph made this statement, "So now it was not you that sent me hither, but God, and He hath made me a father to Pharaoh, and lord of all his house, and a ruler throughout all the land of Egypt" (Gen. 45:8).

Titles Were Accurately Used

This was a statement relating to actual titles — "Father to Pharaoh" meant that Joseph altered the title from "Father to the gods" to "Father to Pharaoh." The pharaoh was supposed to be the manifestation of Ra the Sun God, so Joseph could not use that title, for thereby he would be recognizing pharaoh as God.

The next title was "Lord of Pharaoh's House" — Joseph was in charge of all palace affairs. Then the third title was "Ruler of all Egypt" — both north and south Egypt. (Mizraim — Egypt is a plural word.)

It is interesting to draw a spiritual lesson from those titles. The pharaoh recognized his need for a counselor wiser than himself in administrative matters. We who are Christians likewise need a counselor to help us over those difficult spots — and Jesus is still the Master Counselor.

Joseph Would Not Recognize an Egyptian Pharaoh as "God"

These are gods of various ancient peoples. The prostrate figure in front was a pharaoh — worshiped as the sun-god.

Joseph was lord of pharaoh's house, and our Lord has the right to control HIS house. We recognize His authority in the Church — He himself is LORD of the affairs of the world, and that includes each of us.

And finally Joseph was ruler of all Egypt. As he traveled the land in his chariot the people had to "bow the knee" and call out to him in worship. In a coming day every knee will bow before our Lord, but believing Christians have that privilege even now — and we gladly offer to Him our worship.

Jacob Blesses His Grandsons

In Genesis 48 we read of Jacob blessing the two sons of Joesph — Manasseh and Ephraim. It was normal for the elder son to receive the primary blessing, given by the right hand of the one proclaiming the blessing.

However, Jacob deliberately gave his right-handed blessing to Ephraim, his younger grandson, while blessing Manasseh, the older son, with his left hand. Joseph was displeased at this, and in verse 18 we read his protest that Jacob's right hand should have been placed on the head of the firstborn son.

Jacob Blesses His Grandsons

Jacob insisted that he knew what he was doing, and the blessings remained as he gave them (verses 19 and 20). Later (in chapter 49) Jacob pronounced deathbed blessings and announcements about the future for each of his 12 sons. He was accurate in both incidents of blessing. He was clearly guided by the Holy Spirit of God.

After giving that blessing (taken very seriously in those times) Jacob died — first having secured a promise that he would be buried where Abraham and others of the family had been buried in the Cave of Machpelah at Hebron.

In Genesis 50:2-4 there is a description of the preparations for Jacob to be buried and it is clear that the writer is fully acquainted with Egyptian embalming procedures, mourning customs, and the arrangements made for funerals. These included 40 days for embalming the body and a period of 70 days of mourning for an important person.

In his book, *Ancient Orient and the Old Testament*, Professor Kenneth Kitchen states,

> Burials of Semites and others resident in Egypt are well-attested in the Middle Kingdom ('Abdu at Saqqara: Canaanite cemeteries at Tell el-Dab'a), and this continued in the New Kingdom (Urhiya and others); we find Carians and Greeks likewise in the Late Period.[29]

Genesis 50:7-9 indicates that the courtege was accompanied by high dignitaries, horsemen, and chariots. This also was in accordance with the Egyptian custom of large numbers attending funeral processions to the burial place. (Elaborated by A.S. Yahuda in *The Accuracy of the Bible*.) Thus, it is interesting to read at Genesis 50:11 that the local Canaanites regarded the funeral procession for Jacob as being "a grievous mourning for the Egyptians."

Jacob Was Embalmed . . . Egyptian Practices Were Followed

Eventually Joseph himself died, was embalmed, and put in a coffin in Egypt. Later his bones were carried towards Canaan at the time of the Exodus.

It is a sad commentary that this magnificent Book of Genesis that started with "In the beginning, God . . ." concludes with the note, "In a coffin in Egypt." Sin had intruded — but thank God a new beginning was to follow.

In Many Ways Joseph Pre-figures the Lord Jesus Christ

Joseph was especially loved by his father, as shown by the distinctive coat that was given to him. Jesus also was the anointed Son of His Father, and that special relationship was declared from Heaven with the affirmation, "Thou art my beloved Son in whom I am well-pleased."

Joseph was sold for 20 shekels of silver, the normal price for an able-bodied male slave at that time (Gen. 37:28). Jesus was also sold for the current price of a slave — 30 pieces of silver. In a way, Joseph went into death when he was sold into slavery in Egypt. Jesus actually went into death, even the death of a cross. Joseph was raised to a seat of power, and so was Jesus at the resurrection and His ascension.

The People Had to Bow the Knee to Joseph

Joseph rode in the second chariot of the pharaoh, and an attendant cried before him, "Bow the knee!" In a coming day every knee will bow before the Lord Jesus: it is our privilege to offer Him our ongoing worship through all the days of our lives.

SECTION V

A GREATER-THAN-ALL-THE-MEN-OF-GENESIS IS HERE!

(i) A Greater-than-Adam . . . and Abel . . . and Enoch . . . and Noah Is Here

"Jesus Christ . . . the image of the invisible God (1 Cor. 15:45; Col. 1:15).

Jesus said, "A greater-than-Solomon is here," and "A greater-than-Jonah is here" (Matt. 12:41–42). We want to carry this thought along, for Scripture shows that a greater-than-all-the-great-men-of-the-past is here. In this volume we consider His superiority to the heroes of Genesis.

Adam Was an Actual Man . . . Contrasted with Jesus

We learn in Genesis 1:26, as well as in the New Testament, that Adam was created in the image of God, but as we read on in those early chapters of Genesis we find that Adam sinned. We do not know all the details about that sin, and we do not need to know. We do know that Adam failed when he was tested. In a sense you and I can be seen in this story, for while Adam was a literal person he was also a representative of all men. We can see ourselves in Adam who failed in his test and was shut off from the presence of God. He needed redemption and reconciliation with his Creator, and so do you and I.

Romans 5 makes it clear that Adam was an actual person. He was created in the image of God, and this immediately reminds us of the superiority of our Lord. He was not CREATED in the image of God, for He IS the image of the invisible God.

As David the psalmist reminds us, He was begotten and not created, and as we go through the Scriptures we never find it stated that Jesus Christ was created. He was before all things, and by Him all things consist. The expression, "the first-born of all creation" (Col. 1:15), literally refers to His pre-eminence, NOT to His "creation" as such. He is the One for whom ALL things were created — they were created BY Him and for Him (Col. 1:16). So a greater-than-Adam is here. Adam was created in the image of God, but Jesus Christ is the image of the triune godhead — He has lived eternally, and on earth He was God manifest in flesh. A greater-than-Adam is here.

We have said that when he was tested Adam failed, and he was driven from the presence of God. Jesus Christ was tested in all points as we are, yet without sin. He knew no sin, neither was guile found in His mouth. Even as a man He could have returned to His Father's presence, for on the Mount of Transfiguration we see Him in His glory as the perfect Man, but instead of returning to heaven He came down from that mountain to go on to the Cross, to give himself for us. He went voluntarily to death, even to the death of the Cross, where the face of God was shut off from Him as He died for Adam's helpless race. Adam had been shut off from the face of God, and now the face of God was shut off from Jesus Christ as He went into death. He was forsaken of God and He cried, "My God, why have You forsaken Me?" Why indeed? Because He was taking Adam's place. He was taking MY place.

Adam was given a garden to tend as a place in which he would serve God. Jesus knew what it was to serve God as He became the perfect Servant who went about doing good. The very heavens had seemed to open as the Father proclaimed, "This is My beloved Son in whom I am well pleased." It was pleasing to our Lord to undertake service for His Heavenly Father.

On another day we see Him, not serving in the Garden of Eden but agonizing in the Garden of Gethsemane. There His sweat was as great drops of blood falling to the ground. He knew the spiritual price of going on to the Cross to take the curse which was Adam's just penalty.

Going back to Adam's scene of failure, we learn of pain and subjection, of curse and sorrow, of thorns and sweat of the brow, of death and separation from God while a sword guarded the way to the tree of life. In the New Testament these things are illustrated in the life of the Lord Jesus Christ. As Peter the Apostle said in Acts 2:24, our Lord took on himself the pains of death because He was taking Adam's place. He also took MY place. Adam came into a place of subjection by his own choice when he sinned. Jesus Christ came into a place of subjection when He, by His own choice, did NOT sin, but BECAME sin for us. He took bondage when He himself became subject to death.

Redeemed from the Curse

A curse was placed upon Adam when he failed, but in Galatians 3:13 we read, "Christ has redeemed us from the curse of the law, having become a curse for us (for it is written, 'Cursed is everyone who hangs on a tree')" (NKJV). He took Adam's curse — He took my curse, for the Scriptures tell us that the wages of sin is death.

Eve was told that in sorrow she would bring forth children, for this was part of her judgment. Adam loved her, and sinned knowingly, and together they went forth sorrowing, shut off from the place of blessing. In Isaiah 53:3 we read of one who was "a man of sorrows, and acquainted with grief: and we hid as it were our faces from Him." The Lord Jesus Christ was that man of sorrows who sorrowed unto death.

Adam was told that the ground would be cursed and would bring forth thorns. Matthew 27:29 tells us of one who was crowned with thorns, and the curse was placed upon His head as He took our place, paying the price for our sin. Adam was told that in the sweat of his brow he would eat bread, and in the Garden of Gethsemane we see one whose sweat was as great drops of blood falling to the ground. Jesus Christ was taking the place of Adam and of Adam's helpless race — He would redeem all who would trust Him as substitute and Saviour.

A Sword and a Tree of Life

A sword was placed outside the Garden of Eden to prevent access to the tree of life. If man had partaken of that tree he would have lived forever, but he would have been a failing human being. Imagine someone who could live forever with cancer, and with all the other illnesses that are known to the human race, in a body that could never die, forever tormented and suffering. In the goodness of God, the way to that tree of life was barred until the day came when one went into death to make access to God possible, with a new life in a redeemed body. Even the possibility of cancer will have been removed. We shall have imperishable, immortal bodies (1 Cor. 15:53).

Yes, there was one who said, "I am come that they might have life" (John 10:10), and also, "I am the way, the truth and the life" (John 14:6). Jesus Christ offers life, for He himself went into death. No longer is there a sword to keep us from the tree of life: in the Revelation, the last book of the Bible, we read that access is again open to the tree of life whose leaves are for the healing of the nations (Rev. 22:2).

We have touched on a number of points of comparison and contrast between our Lord and Adam, and it is good to remind ourselves of these spiritual truths. Adam was made in the image of God, but the Lord

Jesus Christ is God, "the image of the invisible God" (Col. 1:15). We cannot see that which is invisible in the natural realm, but He is God. In Him all the fulness of the godhead dwells bodily (Col. 2:9). Adam had dominion over the living creation, and the Lord Jesus Christ said after His death and resurrection, "All authority has been given to Me" (Matt. 28:18). At the end of the first creation God said, "It is very good" (Gen. 1:31). Jesus restored what He "took not away" when He reconciled the world to himself so that there could be a new and perfect creation in His resurrection life.

God saw there was no helpmeet for Adam (Gen. 2:20), and so Adam was put into a deep sleep and his body was rent so that from that body a bride could be formed. There was no "helpmeet" for our Lord, and He, too, went into a deep sleep, the sleep of death. His side was opened so we could become bone of His bone and flesh of His flesh. We who know the Lord Jesus Christ as personal Saviour have become members of His body, part of the bride of Christ. In their state of innocence it is said of Adam and Eve that they were not ashamed, and now the Lord Jesus Christ presents us before His Father, and He is not ashamed to call us brethren (Heb. 2:11).

Adam listened to the voice of the woman and also to the arch-enemy of souls, but the Lord Jesus Christ rebuked the devil when He was tested in the wilderness. Adam blamed another — his wife, but the Lord Jesus Christ, who was without sin, took the sin of His prospective bride upon himself. At the Fall, God said that the serpent would bruise the heel of the seed of the woman, and that that seed would crush the serpent's head. When He died, the "heel" of the Lord Jesus Christ was bruised, but Satan's head was crushed — Calvary ensured the final triumph over sin and death and hell. In sorrow the woman was to bear children, and her sorrow was to be multiplied, but the Lord Jesus Christ was a "Man of sorrows." Though cut off from the land of the living, He would yet see His seed, and be satisfied.

Romans 5:14 tells us that death reigned from Adam to Moses, and now a greater-than-Adam is here. Adam's disobedience led to death, but our Lord's obedience leads us to eternal life. Where Adam could only know death and separation from God, Jesus Christ offers life and eternal fellowship with a loving Heavenly Father.

The Seed of the Woman

Adam and Eve were told that through the seed of the woman the nations would be blessed. Our Lord was that seed of the woman, and blessing is given to the world. Thus we read in Galatians 4:4–6: "When the fullness of time had come, God sent forth His Son, born of a woman, born under the law, to redeem those who were under the law, that we might receive the adoption as sons. And because you are sons, God has sent forth the Spirit of His Son into your hearts, crying out, Abba, Father!"

In 1 Corinthians 15:21 we read that by man came death, for in Adam all die. A greater-than-Adam is here, for though by the man Adam came death, by the Man Jesus Christ comes life. As we study Romans 5 and 1 Corinthians 15, we find this wonderful story told — failure and death through Adam, but glorious redemption and resurrection life through Jesus Christ. In Adam all die, but in Jesus Christ all who know Him as Saviour will live forever. A greater-than-Adam is here.

Abel . . . Enoch . . . and Noah

Adam was not the only early man mentioned in early Genesis, and it is a profitable study to consider how Jesus is superior to others referred to in the early chapters of Genesis. The first baby born, Cain, was a murderer. He killed his brother Abel when Abel's sacrifice of a lamb was acceptable to God, whereas Cain's offering of the fruit of the ground was not acceptable. Abel's blood offering pointed to the Lamb of God whose offering of himself would make it possible for man to be reconciled to God. Cain needed atonement, and it was Jesus who, in the fullness of time, made that atonement possible.

Abel's blood cried out from the ground (Gen. 4:10), calling to God for vengeance. Jesus willingly offered himself to God, and His blood cries out in forgiveness, not vengeance. A greater-than-Abel is here.

Another great man was Enoch, who "walked with God, and he was not, for God took him" (Gen. 5:24) He walked with God — and he was taken when he was 365 years old — as many years as there are days in the year. In a sense Enoch points us to Him who "walked with God" every day of every year for all of time, and on into eternity. A greater-than-Enoch is here.

Noah "found grace in the eyes of the Lord" (Gen. 6:8) when all around him man's wickedness caused God to be "sorry that He had made man on the earth" (Gen. 6:6). Noah and his sons built the ark, and they and their wives were saved. Jesus offered himself as our "ark," the only means whereby men could be safe against the righteous judgment of God against sin. He took its full penalty in His own body.

Later Noah himself failed in an incident involving drunkenness. This indirectly led to his son also sinning and earning the pronouncement of a curse from Noah (Gen. 9:20–27). Jesus never failed, and instead of pronouncing a curse because of drunkenness, He himself became the song of the drunkards (Ps. 69:21), when he died for His spiritual sons on Calvary.

Noah "found grace in the eyes of the Lord," but Jesus was "full of grace and truth" (John 1:14). A greater-than-Noah is here, even He who was with the Father "in the beginning." He became man so that salvation could be offered to all. A greater-than-Adam is here: Jesus, the eternal Son of God.

(ii) A GREATER-THAN-ABRAHAM IS HERE

"Are you greater than our father Abraham?" (John 8:53).

"Before Abraham was — I Am" (John 8:58).

"Are you greater than our father Abraham?" the Jews asked Jesus and the question is recorded in John 8:53. In this meditation we shall give the answer, for a greater-than-Abraham is here, the one who could say, "Before Abraham was, I Am."

To the Jews, Abraham was the father of their faith, and he was indeed a mighty man of God. He obeyed the challenge of God to go forth as a pilgrim and a stranger, leaving behind him the magnificent culture and comfort of Ur, and later of Haran also. Abraham was a man of exceptional character, and he was obedient to the call of God. We see him unselfishly allowing his nephew Lot to choose the way he will go when there is trouble between the herdsmen. We see him as a man of courage as he goes out to rescue that same nephew when Lot had been captured in battle.

We see him as a man of true benevolence toward God as he offers tithes to Melchizedek, the high priest of the living God, as recorded in Genesis 14. We recognize that he is a man who cannot be bribed and who will not stoop to take rewards on wrong terms. Here Abraham said "No!" to the king of Sodom, a wicked king who would have claimed that he had made Abraham rich if he had accepted the payment and gifts offered.

He was a man who knew what it is to intercede for others. When he was told of the destruction of the cities of Sodom and Gomorrah he petitioned the Lord to show mercy when judgment was so over-ripe. When we come to the New Testament, in Hebrews 11:17, we are reminded that he was also a great man of faith. This faith was behind all those other attributes: the character of Abraham stemmed from an elementary rule, the rule of faith towards God.

An Honest Record — Even as to Failure

Yet there are times when we see him fail. Even though to the Jews he was the great father of their race, the Scripture records his failure, too. The Bible does indeed record failures and difficulties, as well as wonderful successes and actions that glorify God. The Bible is a book of truth, and it records the histories of great men truthfully even though this might show an undesirable side of their character. So we see there is another side to the character of Abraham. On one occasion he denied his wife Sarah, risking her honor so that his own life would not be taken. This was when Abraham went down into Egypt, recorded for us in Genesis 12.

Similarly, when Abraham took the girl Hagar he went against the promise which God had given him, even though he acted in accordance with the customs of his times. The Bible records what took place without saying that the action itself was right. Obviously, Abraham should have waited, because the child of promise was yet to be born. The promises of God are sure, even though it might seem they take time to be fulfilled. Eventually Isaac, that child of promise, was born, but because of Abraham's failure and lack of faith Ishmael also had been born, and his descendants have been amongst the greatest opponents to the descendants of Isaac, even to our Lord Jesus Christ who was born in the line of that child of promise.

As we think of Isaac we are reminded of another way in which "a greater-than-Abraham is here." Isaac's birth was miraculous in that Sarah was given special strength when she was past child-bearing age, and our Lord's birth was miraculous, for He was born of a virgin — He had no earthly father as you and I have a father. HE was the Son of God and when HE was born in Bethlehem a greater-than-Abraham was here. He was Emmanuel, God with us.

The Jews Are Startled!

Referring again to John 8, the time came when the Lord Jesus Christ told those who would question Him, that Abraham had seen His day and rejoiced. Can you just see those Jews looking at each other, and then back in amazement to the remarkable Man in their midst? Yet Abraham did indeed see the day of the Lord Jesus Christ: he saw it when the angel of the Lord came to Abraham's tent before the cities of Sodom and Gomorrah were destroyed.

That story is told in Genesis 18 where we read that the Lord appeared to Abraham in the Plains of Mamre. As Abraham sat at the door of the tent in the heat of the day, three men appeared and Abraham acted as their host. Possibly this is the incident referred to in Hebrews 13:2 where we read, "Do not forget to entertain strangers, for by so doing some have unwittingly entertained angels."

An Old Testament Christophany

Clearly one of those three was superior to the others: He took to himself the name of the Lord, in verses 13, 14, 17, etc. This is one of those incidents referred to by some scholars as Christophanies, appearances of our Lord in Old Testament times. In these appearances the Lord often takes to himself the title of the "Angel of the Lord" and is prepared to accept the homage of men. No created being should accept such worship, and a study of these appearances makes it clear that this one is not a created being, but is God himself.

It is not our purpose to study the Christophanies as such, but we mention in passing that other instances are found in Genesis 16:7, Joshua 5:13, Judges 6:11, Judges 13:2 — and at other places.

At first sight it might seem strange that in this particular appearance of the Lord there are two quite opposite revelations to Abraham. The first is that Sarah is to give birth to a child when she is past the normal age of childbearing, and the second is that the cities of Sodom and Gomorrah are to be destroyed.

Thus, in this one visitation there is the promise of life and there is the declaration of coming judgment on those who reject the Lord. There is a spiritual illustration in this, for the coming of Christ means both life and death — life to the believer, and spiritual death to those who reject the grace of God.

This is not unlike the implication of the apostle Paul's statement in 2 Corinthians 2:15-16, "For we are to God the fragrance of Christ among those who are being saved and among those who are perishing. To the one we are the aroma of death to death, and to the other the aroma of life to life."

At first we are not entirely aware that this is the Lord himself, and it seems that Abraham also did not know who his guest was. Abraham's actions are those of a typical Eastern host, and so we watch as he has water fetched for the washing of his guest's feet, and as Sarah prepares an appetizing meal. Then we begin to notice something different. Abraham is asked, "Where is Sarah your wife?" (Gen. 18:9). We find ourselves wondering how this visitor knew the name of Abraham's wife, and soon we learn that this one is the Son of God.

Sarah Laughed

Sarah was in the tent and she heard the Lord say that she was to have a son. She laughed, for, humanly speaking, it was impossible for her to bear a child. "Why did Sarah laugh?" the Lord asked Abraham, and went on to ask that question often repeated since, "Is anything too hard for the Lord?" Through the ages many a saint has found that the "impossible" can be accomplished when that "impossible" is required for the glory of God. Again we read in Mark 10:27, "With men it is impossible, but not with God: for with God all things are possible."

Through the Scriptures there are many illustrations of the "impossible" being accomplished when faith was directed toward the all-powerful God. The River Jordan could open miraculously; the walls of Jericho could fall down at the appointed time; the lions' mouths could be stopped when Daniel was in their den; and the prison could be opened in the days of Peter. The Christian who is in the will of God can know that nothing is too hard for the Lord, that all things are made to work together for good to them that love God, to those who are called according to His purpose (Rom. 8:28).

The Lord promised Abraham and Sarah that she would bear a son, and soon after that the men rose up and set out towards Sodom. Then we listen as the Lord says, "Shall I hide from Abraham what I am doing?" (Gen. 18:17). Thus, Abraham was brought into the privileged place of knowing about the judgment to be visited on the wicked cities of Sodom and Gomorrah. The Lord said, "Their sin is very grievous" (Gen. 18: 20), and in a similar way the Christian today is brought into the confidence of his Lord. He, too, knows that judgment is to be visited on the world because its sin is also very grievous.

Interceding with the Judge of All the Earth

The two men with the Lord went on their way, but we read in verse 22, "But Abraham still stood before the Lord." Here we have a very wonderful spiritual principle, for Abraham is able to stand in the presence of "the judge of all the earth" and to intercede for the inhabitants of the wicked cities. Abraham was all too conscious that his nephew Lot was living in one of the cities of vice, and his heart would have been heavy as he realized that Lot would be involved in this judgment. Abraham knew that Lot had acted foolishly, but the modern saying that "blood is thicker than water" was surely just as true in Abraham's day as it is today. Abraham had already risked his life to rescue Lot when he was captured by those who attacked the city of Sodom.

Although Lot had soon returned to his adopted city, no doubt Abraham had Lot in mind as he stood before the Lord. The Christian today has the privilege of standing before the Lord and interceding for loved ones and for others who are in spiritual Sodoms or Gomorrahs. Constantly the Christian is enjoined to pray without ceasing, and one of the functions of prayer is that of intercession — pleading for another, as though we were putting ourselves in the place of that other.

Abraham besought the Lord to spare the city for the sake of 50 righteous within the city of Sodom. The Lord said that He would not slay the city if there were 50 righteous. Abraham knew it was the Lord he was addressing, for he said, "Shall not the Judge of all the earth do right?" (Gen. 18:25).

"Perhaps there will be 5 less than 50," Abraham said. "Would You destroy all of the city for lack of 5?" Again the Lord said that He would not destroy it if there were 45 persons. Abraham came to 40, and then to 30, to 20, and then at last to 10. "I will not destroy it for the sake of 10," said the Lord. Then we read in verse 33, "And the Lord went His way as soon as He had finished speaking with Abraham; and Abraham returned to his place."

But a greater-than-Abraham is here. Abraham stopped when he reached the figure of 10, but our Lord did not. He knew that 10 righteous men could not be found in all the earth, for there was none righteous, no, not one (Rom. 3:10). As the apostle Paul later put it, "For all have sinned, and fall short of the glory of God" (Rom. 3:23).

The Lord Jesus Christ himself was righteous, the only man who ever lived who could claim to be sinless. And so He did not stop at ten, but came down to one, and that one was himself.

The world can be spared because one righteous man was found, even the Lord Jesus Christ. We read, "He is also able to save to the uttermost those who come to God through Him, since He ever lives to make intercession for them" (Heb. 7:25). A greater-than-Abraham is here.

Life and Death Foretold and Fulfilled

We mentioned that associated with this Christophany — this Old Testament appearance of Christ — was the promise of a child to Abraham and Sarah, and the warning of judgment against the cities of the plain. In due time both events were brought to pass, for Sarah did indeed bear a son, even Isaac, the child of promise. And Sodom and Gomorrah were destroyed, just as the Lord had said would come to pass. Life and death were each foretold, and each came to pass.

So probably our Lord thought of that scene in the Plains of Mamre when He told the Jews, "Abraham rejoiced to see My day, and he saw it and was glad." Today we who are by faith the spiritual sons of Abraham continue rejoicing because we, too, have seen His day. We know that the Christ child, even Jesus the child has been born. And we know that though our sin also was very grievous, yet Jesus Christ has taken this judgment upon himself. The judge of the earth has done right — not only has He pronounced judgment against our sin, but He has borne its penalty to the full. Abraham interceded but for a moment, and then returned to his place. Our Lord ever lives to make intercession for us.

A Greater-Than-Abraham Is Here

Jesus is the Son of God, and He lives eternally — He lived before He was born in Bethlehem. So the Lord Jesus Christ said that Abraham saw His day and rejoiced. The Jews challenged Him when He said this, and said that He was not yet 50 years of age, so how could Abraham have seen His day?

Abraham was only a man, even though a wonderful man. Jesus Christ the eternal one is beyond time, and He was with His Heavenly Father before Abraham was born. When He said, "Before Abraham was, I am," He was saying that He is the ever living one, one who is ever present, the great "I Am." Abraham was but for a moment. He passed across the stage of history, and soon he was known only in the records and in his posterity. But Jesus Christ IS the same yesterday, and today, and for ever. So He could say, "Before Abraham was, I am." Truly, a greater-than-Abraham is here.

"Nowhere to Lay His Head"

Jesus Christ was greater than Abraham in what He gave up. Abraham left the magnificence of that culture of Mesopotamia, but Jesus left the glories of heaven — to go to the cross of Calvary. Abraham was a pilgrim and a stranger with his God, but he became a rich man. On the other hand our Lord could say, "The foxes have holes and the birds of the air have nests, but the Son of Man has nowhere to lay His head" (Matt. 8:20). Abraham denied his own wife rather than risk his life, but Jesus Christ gave His life because only by giving that life could His bride be purchased for himself.

Abraham at times went outside the will of God, and we see this especially as he went down into Egypt in a time of distress. He had to come back to Bethel, that place which meant "house of God" (Gen. 13:1–4). Jesus Christ never knew what it was to backslide for, as His own disciples have declared to us, "He knew no sin, neither was guile found in His mouth." When Mary and Joseph chided Him after they came back and found Him in the temple at 12 years of age, He told them, "Did you not know that I must be about My Father's house?" (Luke 2:49). He ever was in the will of God: He ever was, spiritually, in Bethel the house of God.

Abraham failed when he took to himself Hagar from whom Ishmael was born. Abraham should have waited for that child of promise. In the course of time God honored His promise that Sarah would give birth to a son, and Isaac was born. Through him all the nations of the earth were to be blessed, and this has been especially fulfilled through the Lord Jesus Christ who was a Son of Isaac according to human genealogy.

The greatest test of Abraham's life was when God challenged him to offer his son of promise on Mount Moriah. Abraham obeyed, believing that God could, and would, raise his son to life again. As Abraham's hand was raised and he was about to slay Isaac, the Lord called to him, and Isaac was spared. Then Abraham sacrificed a ram that was caught in a nearby thicket (Gen. 22:13).

Isaac had asked, "My father . . . where is the lamb for a burnt offering?" and Abraham had answered, "My son, God will provide for himself the lamb for a burnt offering" (Gen. 22:7-8). Abraham was prepared to offer his own son because he expected God to raise Isaac from the dead (Heb. 11:19), but God accepted Abraham's faith without the actual sacrifice. Jesus fulfilled the embodiment of this sacrifice, and God did provide himself a lamb. "God was in Christ, reconciling the world to himself" (2 Cor. 5:19). This was a much greater happening than what Abraham was involved in. God DID offer His own Son, and Jesus WAS raised from the dead. A greater-than-Abraham, and a greater-than-Isaac, was here, even the eternal and only begotten Son of God.

A greater-than-Abraham was here, for on the third day He rose again, victorious over sin, and death, and hell. He laid down His life, and He took it up again as He rose from the dead. In Hebrews 11 we are reminded that Abraham looked for a city whose builder and maker was God, but he did not find it until he had passed from this life. Jesus Christ himself came to give us this city of the living God. He said, "In My Father's house are many mansions: I go to prepare a place for you" (John 14:2). He went into death so that fellowship with God could be restored, so that we could again live in the presence of God. All this is found in the person of the Lord Jesus Christ.

Christ Is Risen!

Abraham died, and they buried him in the cave of Machpelah. Jesus Christ died, and they buried Him in a new tomb wherein no man had ever laid. On the third day He rose from the dead, for death could not hold Him — He laid down His life and He took it again in resurrection. A greater-than-Abraham is here, the one who could say, "Before Abraham was, I Am." This is Jesus Christ, the same yesterday and today and forever, one who lives eternally. He still says to each of us, "Behold I stand at the door of your heart and knock. May I come in?" Jesus is challenging us to a spiritual pilgrimage, and assuring us of HIS presence in the wilderness.

Isaac eventually took to himself a bride, Rebekah, "and Isaac was comforted after his mother's death" (Gen. 24:67). Jesus also took to himself a bride, His church, and now He, too, is comforted after His own death. Man had sinned, and so had earned the penalty of death. Jesus loved the Church, His bride, and died for her. He rose from the dead victorious, and now He rejoices to call those who believe in Him His friends, His Church, His bride.

Rebekah personally chose to become the bride of Isaac (Gen. 24:58), and as we "go forth to Him, outside the camp" (Heb. 13:13) we find that He is the altogether lovely one. The greatest of all men is here. We shall love Him and serve Him forever.

(iii) A GREATER-THAN-JACOB IS HERE

"Are you greather than our father Jacob?" (John 4:12).

One day a Samaritan woman at Jacob's well asked Jesus, "Are You greater than our father Jacob?" (John 4:12). He told her He could provide her with living water, instead of the ordinary water she came to draw from this well made by the patriarch Jacob.

Our immediate interest is in her question, "Are You greater than our father Jacob?" Jesus told her He was the Messiah, using the expression, *Ego Eimi*, "I, even I, Am." That was a title of divinity, and sometimes it was blasphemously used of false gods.

One way in which Christ's deity is shown is by the use of this term. This is an emphatic use of the personal pronoun "I." The word *eimi* in Greek is sufficient to say "I am," this being the first person present active of the verb "to be." But added to this in John's gospel is the personal pronoun *ego* — "I." Thus, we are told that our Lord said, "I, even I, AM" — *ego eimi*. (Once again a concept known in current language is given a new spiritual significance. This can be demonstrated at many places in the Scriptures, as with some of the Psalms of David.)

The expression *ego eimi* was known as "sacred" language when John wrote his gospel. Here is one famous inscription about the Egyptian goddess Isis:

I am Isis, the queen of every land, taught by Hermes, and whatsoever things I have ordained, no one is able to loose them. I am the eldest daughter of Cronos, the youngest god. I am wife and sister of King Osiris. I am the first that devised fruit for men. I am mother of Horus the King. I am she that riseth in the dog-star.

Over and over again in that inscription Isis is made to use this sacred expression, *ego eimi*. The inscription shows how Satan takes the things of God and gives them a false meaning. There is only one who in truth can take to himself this title "I AM," for this is the title of God himself. It was the name of God as revealed to Moses in Exodus 3:14 — "I Am that I Am." At the same time Moses was instructed to tell the people that "I Am" had sent him to them.

Jesus took to himself that divine title. This same teaching is reflected in the term He used when He compared himself with Abraham. "Before Abraham was, I Am," He told the Jews (John 8:58). Abraham "was" — he appeared for a brief moment on the scene of Bible history and then moved on. In contrast, Jesus Christ could say "I AM" — the one who always is, the only one who could say, "Before Abraham was, I AM." He is the true "I AM," the ever-living Son of God.

When the officers came to arrest Jesus He asked them, "Whom are you seeking?" (John 18:4). They said, "Jesus of Nazareth," and He merely said, *Ego Eimi* — "I Am." At this they fell to the ground, and the Lord repeated His question. To their answer He replied, "I have told you that I Am." As we watch them fall down we realize that mere men could not so much as touch the Son of God until He allowed it. "Therefore, if you seek Me, let these go their way," He commanded. How strange — the prisoner was allowing himself to be taken, but demanding that His disciples (who had publicly identified themselves with His teaching and way of life) should go unharmed! Strange, and yet true.

And Jesus used those same words on a number of occasions. He said, "I Am — the door;" "I Am — the Good Shepherd;" "I Am — the vine;" "I Am — the way, the truth, and the life;" "I Am — the resurrection and the life." When He said to that Samaritan woman, *Ego Eimi* (the Messiah), He was using that title and by implication He was indeed "greater than Jacob."

That superiority can be demonstrated in special ways from the records about Jacob himself in the Book of Genesis. As we consider his life we find similarities to Jesus, but Jesus is greatly superior. Jacob's conflicts between his self-centered nature and his higher desires are well-known. Jesus knew no such conflict, but even in the agony of the Garden of Gethsemane He could declare, "Not My will, but Yours, be done" (Luke 22:42).

The Elder Shall Serve the Younger

In Genesis 25 we are told before the birth of Esau and Jacob that the elder brother Esau would serve his younger brother Jacob. The principle of divine election is here indicated. In Malachi 1 it is clearly stated that Esau was unacceptable to God, and his descendants knew the judgment of God. In Romans 9 it is again made clear that God chose Jacob and rejected Esau.

In this incident in Genesis 25 we begin to see something of God's sovereignty, but we also see something of His omniscience, for this election by God has been proved by history to be justified. God knew all the circumstances, and by their later lives Jacob and Esau showed just how right God was.

Humanly speaking, it first seemed most unlikely that Esau WOULD serve Jacob, for Esau was a hunter, a courageous man who loved to be on the trail of wild animals. In addition he was his father's favorite. On the other hand, Jacob was a shepherd and stayed around the home more than his adventurous brother. As Esau was his father's favorite son, so Jacob was the favorite of his mother, Rebekah.

Esau Sells His Birthright

This young man who was ready to stay at home was also a man of ambition, and he was prepared to use cunning to gain the birthright which in those days was so very important. He wanted that birthright, and he set out to get it. One day he had his opportunity. Esau came home, weary from the hunt, and Jacob had made a tasty meal. Esau asked for some of it, and Jacob took the opportunity to demand that in return Esau sell his birthright. Esau agreed, saying he was even then at the point of death. Then Jacob made him swear by an oath to confirm that the birthright really had been handed over. As the Bible says, "Thus Esau despised his birthright."

(In passing we mention that there is a well-known story from the excavations at Nuzi where a man sold a grove for three sheep. It reminds us of this record about Jacob and Esau.)

So Jacob cheated his brother Esau out of his birthright. God had promised it to Jacob, but Jacob went ahead of God, and gained it by underhanded means (Gen. 25: 29–34). Esau "despised his birthright" and demonstrated the reality of God's foreknowledge. In His wisdom God decreed that Jacob would take over the rights of the first-born. However, that did not justify Jacob denying food to his brother when he was exhausted. Jacob acted outside the will of God, and because of this he had to flee for his life. Part of the price of his deception was that he never saw his mother again.

"I Restored What I Did Not Take"

Contrast all this with Jesus. It is written prophetically of Him in Psalm 69:4, "Though I have stolen nothing, I still must restore it." The right of the first-born was His eternally, for He is the eternal Son of God. He Who knew no sin paid the price of sin; He who is the author of life went into death; He redeemed those who had lost their spiritual birthright because of sin; He has restored our heritage, and now we are "heirs of God, and joint-heirs with Christ" (Rom. 8:17).

Jacob gained the birthright of his brother at the wrong time, through cheating his brother, and then deceiving his father (Gen. 27:1–29). Cheating and deceit are sin.

Jesus restored the birthright to us, His brethren, at the very time that God had appointed (Gal. 4:4). In contrast to Jacob deceiving his father, Jesus delighted to do His Father's will. Jesus' actions involved no sin, for He put away sin by the sacrifice of himself (Heb. 9:26).

Jacob and his mother conspired to deceive the aged Isaac, when he was almost blind and they each paid the penalty, for Jacob's swift departure meant that these two never saw each other again. Jacob reaped the result of his own sinful actions.

One of His closest friends wrote that Jesus "committed no sin, nor was guile found in His mouth" (1 Pet. 2:22). Peter lived and worked with Him, knowing Him intimately, yet he declared His sinlessness. Undoubtedly, a greater-than-Jacob is here. Jacob deceived his father, whereas by His death Jesus totally paid for the sins of others.

A Ladder into Heaven

On the way to Haran, after fleeing from home, Jacob had a dream in which he saw a ladder set on the earth and reaching into heaven. In his dream he saw the angels of God ascending and descending and heard the Lord telling him that the covenant made with Abraham and Isaac would be confirmed through him, Jacob.

Jesus also knew the ministration of angels in His life (Luke 22:43; John 1:51). Possibly Jesus had this incident with Jacob in mind when He said to Nathaniel, "Hereafter you shall see heaven open, and the angels of God ascending and descending upon the Son of Man" (John 1:51).

We are reminded of the Lord Jesus in a number of ways in this incident, for He bridged the gap between earth and heaven when He was lifted up to die on a wooden cross. Jacob could not climb that ladder into heaven, but Jesus has now opened the way into the holiest of all, into heaven itself. As the writer to the Hebrews puts it, He has consecrated a new and living way for us through the veil, that is to say, His flesh.

Going back to Jacob, Jacob awoke out of his sleep, and said, "Surely the Lord is in this place, and I did not know it." Jacob further said, "How awesome is this place! This is none other than the house of God, and this is the gate of heaven."

Jacob at Bethel, "House of God"

The name of that place therefore became Bethel, instead of its former name of Luz (Gen. 28:19), for Bethel means "house of God." Spiritually, we are reminded that Jacob did not know the "house of God" until then, and again we are reminded of Jesus. Even at 12 years of age He was busy in His Father's house, and in fact He told Mary and Joseph that He must be busy about His Father's house (Luke 2:49). All His life He sought the things of God.

"This is the gate of heaven," Jacob said. Jesus said of himself, "I am the door." Jesus was also the Good Shepherd, and the two pictures are linked, for the good shepherd was prepared to guard his sheep with his life. In the east the sheep would be put in the fold at night. It had only one entrance, and there the shepherd lay down to sleep so that no animal could go in or out without going over his body. The Good Shepherd was himself the door.

Jesus went on to say that no man could come to the Father but by Him. The door has been opened into the very presence of God. Jacob was at the place which he said was the gate of heaven, and we are at the gate of heaven when we come to Calvary's cross and worship at the feet of Him who was crucified there.

From Luz (Twisting) to Bethel (House of God)

Jacob rose early in the morning and poured oil on the stones as an act of worship. After that experience with God he must rise early to worship Him, and we read that this is associated with oil. In Scripture oil is a symbol of the Holy Spirit, and we are again reminded of Jesus meeting the Samaritan woman by a well. He told her, "God is a Spirit, and those who worship Him must worship Him in spirit and truth" (John 4:24).

The symbolism of the oil reminds us of our God-given capacity to worship God, for the Lord Jesus told His disciples that all believers would be indwelt by the Holy Spirit of God. Each of us now has the capacity to worship in spirit and in truth, for the Holy Spirit indwells us, and each true Christian is a temple of the living God.

We saw that Jacob changed the name of that place from Luz to Bethel (Gen. 28:19). Luz means bending or twisting, and Bethel means house of God. That is a lovely picture, for at that place where the oil was poured a remarkable change took place. In the spiritual realm today it is just as true, for where the oil of the Holy Spirit is applied remarkable changes will take place in all those who have become temples of the Holy Spirit. Our twisting, bending natures are changed, and instead we become houses of God, places where the power of the indwelling Holy Spirit God is known, for He is willing to take up residence in us. Luz, "bending," has given place to Bethel, the house of God.

Jacob's Conditional Prayer

Jacob went on to make a vow before the Lord. He vowed, "If God will be with me, and keep me in this way that I am going, and give me bread to eat, and clothing to put on, so that I come back to my father's house in peace; then the Lord shall be my God." He promised the Lord a tenth of all that He gave him (Gen. 28:22). In some ways this prayer is too conditional, and later in Genesis Jacob came to a place of greater consecration where he did not use the word "IF" as a condition to serving the Lord.

Let us consider the spiritual principles in this verse. Jacob wanted God to be with him, and He is ever anxious to find such a man. He is willing to reveal himself to, and to go with, all those who choose to walk with Him. Spiritually this is just as true today as it was physically in the days of His life on earth.

Jesus makes it a far more real experience than Jacob ever knew. Jacob wanted God to give him bread to eat, and this points to the wonderful provision in the spiritual realm. Jesus could feed thousands of people on more than one occasion from just a handful, for little is much if God is in it. And Jesus is still able to nourish us with spiritual food that will satisfy our spiritual needs entirely. He is the bread of God, and we are still invited to eat of Him.

In the same way, Jacob wanted an assurance that God would give him raiment to put on, and in the spiritual realm we have a raiment that is all-sufficient. Christ offers us a robe of righteousness, a white robe purchased by His shed blood. When we put on that garment of righteousness we find that it is also a wedding garment, and we are invited to the marriage supper of the Lamb. God sees us as those whose sins are covered: for Christ himself is made unto us righteousness.

Some Comparisons and Contrasts

Jacob wanted to come again to his father's house in peace. Historically, that became true many years later, and just as surely it will be true of us spiritually. We, too, left the Father's house, and we were as prodigals. We were as those who had been cast out of a beautiful garden, but now one has made peace by the blood of His cross, and access to the Father is again available. He said, just before He endured that cross, "I go to prepare a place for you."

The way back to the father's house would be accomplished for Jacob in peace, and in the spiritual realm it is even more true. The way back is open, for the Prince of Peace has come, and He has made peace for us by the blood of His cross. Now we who love Him can know peace with God — peace which passes understanding.

Jacob longed for oneness with God, but Jesus and His Father were one (John 10:30). Jacob wanted to receive passing material blessings such as food and raiment, but Jesus gives spiritual blessings that will satisfy through eternity. A greater-than-Jacob is here.

Jacob chose his bride from a people far from home at that time when he was compelled to flee for his life (Gen. 27:41; 28:1–5). Jesus chose His bride from a people "far off," and He "made them nigh" by the blood of His cross (Eph. 2:13). The previous verses (Eph. 2:11–12) remind us that we were Gentiles in times past, without Christ, aliens from the Commonwealth of Israel, strangers from the covenant of promise. In Christ all that is changed, for we are now "the bride of Christ" (Eph. 5:25–27, 32).

The Angel of the Lord Wrestles with Jacob

In Genesis 32 we read of the angel of the Lord wrestling with Jacob. Another interesting thing recorded here is that the angels of God met Jacob as he returned to the land. This reminds us of another scene. The Lord Jesus said there is joy in the presence of the angels over one sinner who repents. Here is Jacob coming back to the Promised Land, the land where God would have him dwell, for God had called Abraham to come into this Promised Land and to remain there. As Jacob goes back, the angels of God meet him. In a way this is a picture of a repentant sinner as he returns home to the Father, with joy in the presence of the angels.

After a time of soul-searching because he is about to face his brother Esau, from whom he had stolen the blessing, Jacob has a remarkable experience. In Genesis 32:24–32 we read that wonderful account of the angel of God wrestling with Jacob. It was not primarily that Jacob wrestled with the angel of God, but that the angel of God wrestled with him. God was over-ruling Jacob's self-interest — overcoming that old nature, and breaking down the opposition within Jacob himself. Eventually, Jacob became helpless and ceased to strive. Instead, he clung to God, and blessings followed.

He now received a three-fold blessing, for in verses 28 to 30 we find he has a new character, a new power, and a new experience. The man whose name was Jacob (supplanter) had a new name — he was now Israel (Prince of God), a prince who had prevailed with God.

In verse 30 we read that Jacob said, "I have seen God face to face," and he called the name of that place Peniel. There was glory all around him as well as within. Jacob had been changed to Israel, and we who were unregenerate, far away from God, have also been given a new name: we have been given the name of Christian. We have taken the name of Christ into our own experience, and now we, too, know glory without and glory within.

The Mark of the Man — and "the Angel of the Lord"

Another delightful point concerns Jacob's walk from that time on. After that incident he walked with a limp. The man — the angel of the Lord — had touched him, and Jacob could never be the same again. If you and I have been touched by the glory of the Lord, if we have seen His glory — if we have known "His sufferings and the glories that should follow" (1 Pet. 1:11) — we, too, will never be the same again. Like Jacob, we have been touched by the man, and our "walk" will be different.

It is, of course, widely believed that this was a "Christophany," an appearance of Christ in Old Testament times. Remember, Jesus LIVED before He was born in Bethlehem, and Scripture makes that quite clear. For example, John 1 tells us that He was with the Father "in the beginning." Micah 5:2 reminds us that His goings forth were from old times.

There are other Old Testament appearances of this heavenly one who many believe was actually our blessed Lord. There was the appearance to Joshua as the captain of the host; there was the revelation to Manoah and his wife concerning the birth of their son Samson; and in Isaiah 6 we read of Isaiah seeing the glory of the Lord.

Compare that with John 12:41, and we hear the Lord himself saying that it was His own glory that Isaiah saw. Our Lord DID show something of His glory, something of the power associated with the glory of the godhead, in Old Testament times. He appeared to Jacob and we continue to recognize that a greater-than-Jacob is here.

We, today, have seen His glory in a much fuller way. We have journeyed with Peter and James and John to the Mount of Transfiguration, and we have beheld His glory. We are changed into His image, from glory to glory, by the Lord the Spirit (2 Cor. 3:18). And we shall share His glory, for He himself in prayer stated that the glory the Father had given Him was given to us (John 17:22).

Much more could be said in consideration of Jacob's character, but it would be beyond our immediate purpose. Jacob reminds us of the sovereign grace of God, chosen before he was born. He points to the omniscience of God, for the man certainly seemed unlikely material to accomplish the purposes of God: God knew His man, for He knows the end from the beginning. Jacob illustrates the possibility of a great spiritual change taking place in a man whose early life suggested no such potential — and we failing mortals therefore take courage!

A greater-than-Jacob is here, for Jesus is himself the sovereign Son of God, omniscient and omnipotent. He has chosen US before the foundation of the world (Eph. 1:4). He is able "to save to the uttermost those who come to God through Him, since He ever lives to make intercession for them" (Heb. 7:25). Jacob needed transforming grace, and that transforming power is available for all who come to Christ by faith. A greater-than-Jacob is here.

Towards the end of Jacob's life we read of other interesting events that have spiritual significance.

The Blessings of Jacob, and the First-Born

In Genesis 48 Joseph heard that his father was ill and he hurried to see him. He took with him his two sons, Ephraim and Manasseh, and Jacob was very pleased to see the visitors. He declared to Joseph that the two boys would be counted as Jacob's own sons. So it is that Joseph is not counted by name among the tribes of Israel, but each of his two sons has his name given to a tribe. Joseph was thus granted a double portion of blessing by his father, for in ancient times the double portion was the right of the first-born, and so in a sense Joseph was given the first-born's place. Though not the eldest son, he was the spiritual leader: even in his earlier dreams it had been made clear that the rest of the family would bow down before him.

We who are Christians have the blessing of the first-born, even the blessing of Jesus Christ himself, the pre-eminent one (Col. 1:18). As Paul reminds us, we are blessed with all spiritual blessings in the heavenlies in Christ (Eph. 1:3). This special act of blessing must have been quite significant in the minds of the two boys concerned. They were thus reminded that their prospects were not primarily as sons of the prime minister or secretary of state of Egypt. Their inheritance and blessings lay with the people of God, not with the mighty, ruling Egyptians.

Jacob's Blessing Was Prophetic

As he gave his blessing, Jacob deliberately put his right hand on the younger son, and in this way signified that the younger son would be more important than the older brother. Jacob's blessing was prophetic, and was quite remarkably fulfilled, for the history of the chosen people, Israel, shows that the tribe of Ephraim certainly did become more powerful than that of Manasseh.

Joseph was not pleased at Jacob's action, but Jacob insisted that he was right. When we come to his later blessings of his other sons, we find that he again displayed remarkable insight, for his prophecies were accurately fulfilled in the history of the tribes that sprang from his sons. His utterances were inspired by the Holy Spirit of God. Jacob insisted on maintaining the changed order of blessing, and we find that men of God whose stories are told in Scripture quite rightly insist on a particular course of action, even though humanly speaking it seems wrong. We can learn from this, for today the Spirit of God can still guide us, and when this happens later events will prove that the Spirit was leading, even though men may have misjudged.

The Natural Gives Place to the Spiritual

There are several examples in Genesis of the first-born child being passed over in favor of a later son. Seth became the leader of the godly line, instead of Cain. Genesis 10:21 indicates that Japheth was Noah's first son, yet Shem was the one through whom the covenant people were to descend.

Abraham, the son of Terah, was chosen instead of his older brother Haran, and Isaac was chosen instead of Ishmael. Jacob himself was chosen instead of his slightly older twin brother, Esau.

In these examples we again see something of the sovereignty of God, for according to the human order the eldest son would have been chosen in each case. The natural line gave place to the spiritual.

However, the divine order is shown to be correct by the history of each of the individuals concerned. Adam's first-born was a murderer, and though the others who were passed over may not have been guilty of that particular sin, they did not display the character to be expected of one chosen by God for such a privileged role.

Jacob's Dying Blessings

In Genesis 49 we come to the death-bed of Jacob, and in a most impressive scene he gathered his sons around him and addressed each one in turn. Once again it is remarkable to see just how accurate were the prophecies concerning these sons of Jacob, and again we are impressed with the fact that Jacob spoke by divine inspiration.

The tribe of Reuben was to become comparatively obscure. Simeon was to be scattered through Israel and was to become one of the weakest tribes. Levi was to be divided in Israel. The tribe of Judah was to increase in strength until the time of the Messiah. Zebulun was to settle in the coastal areas and to engage in trade. Thus, Jacob outlined the history of Israel, tribe after tribe, and each of his prophecies has been fulfilled in minute detail.

Not only did Jacob speak concerning the great nation which would spring from those gathered round his bedside, but he also made wonderful statements concerning the Messiah. Perhaps the best-known of these is in verse 10 where we find that the sceptre of authority would come from the tribe of Judah.

From Judah the great peacemaker would come — for Shiloh, to whom Jacob referred, means "peace bringer." "To Him shall the gathering of the people be," said Jacob.

How right he was, for the lion of the tribe of Judah was Jesus Christ, the Jewish Messiah, and the Saviour of the world. He it was who made peace by the blood of His cross. He is Shiloh, the peace giver, even as He declared to His own disciples — "My peace I give to you" (John 14:27).

Jesus Has Given Us the Blessing of the First-Born

Again we are reminded that a greater-than-Jacob is here. Jacob pronounced these blessings because God so inspired Him. Jesus himself has given us the blessings of the first-born because of His own death. Jacob looked on through the centuries and pointed to the Messiah, but Jesus himself was that Messiah. He was not only the son of Jacob but was in very truth the Son of God.

Jacob died, and in Genesis 50 we have the record of the embalming of his body. The people of Egypt mourned for him the same way they would have done for a member of the royal family of Egypt.

Jesus also died, and there was great mourning for Him. However, His body was not embalmed, for

He did not see corruption. In this, once again, prophecy was fulfilled (Ps. 16:10; Acts 13:35–37). He was not "like" a member of a royal family, for He himself is the King of kings. (1 Tim. 6:15). To Him all men will ultimately "bow the knee" (Phil. 2:10).

A greater-than-Jacob is here.

(iv) A GREATER-THAN-JOSEPH IS HERE

"Every knee shall bow . . . Jesus Christ is Lord" (Phil. 2:9–11).

There are very interesting lessons to be learned from the life of Joseph, and his life reveals remarkable similarities to that of our Lord. Possibly no other man in the whole of Scripture prefigures Him in so many ways.

Joseph's Inherited Characteristics

In the Bible records more is recorded about Joseph than there is about any other patriarch. He himself combines many of the best qualities of his ancestors. We find him as a very able chief minister in Egypt, and we are reminded of the ability of his great-grandfather Abraham. But for all his ability we never find him pushing himself, and we are somewhat reminded of the quietness of his grandfather Isaac. Then again, Joseph is well able to size up a situation and to see the right way to deal with a difficulty — perhaps he had something of the best side of his clever father, Jacob.

We never hear of Joseph being jealous or cruel as most of his brothers proved to be. His character was quite in contrast to theirs, and he showed a far greater understanding of spiritual principles, proving that he was the right man for the work God called him to do.

Quite early in Joseph's life God revealed to him in a dream that the rest of his family would bow down before him. This became literally true in later years when Joseph was the vizier, the chief minister of Egypt. The dreams of Joseph as to his future greatness intensified the hatred Joseph's brothers had for him, and the time came when they seized the opportunity to be rid of their brother forever, or so they thought.

Despised by His Brothers

The first scheme of the brothers was to murder Joseph when he came to them with food. Instead, they accepted Reuben's alternative plan of leaving him in a deep pit nearby, an empty well. While Joseph was lying in that empty well, stripped of the splendid coat which had been the special sign of his father's favor, the brothers sat down and ate their bread. Possibly it was even the bread which Joseph had so willingly brought to them from home.

That reminds us of the scene at Calvary. Joseph had been insulted. Jesus Christ was also insulted and stripped of His robe and, while He suffered, callous soldiers sat down and cast dice to see who would take it. As His own people mocked Him He cried, "Father, forgive them, for they do not know what they do" (Luke 23:34). What an amazing demonstration of His teaching on forgiveness!

We notice, too, the hypocrisy of Joseph's brothers, in Genesis 37:27. They decided to sell him into slavery so that their own hands would not be upon him. Going on through the centuries we find similar hypocrisy at the trial of Jesus Christ, for in John 18:28 we learn that the Jews were falsely demanding the death penalty but would not themselves go into the judgment hall, "lest they should be defiled." What utter hypocrisy! Joseph's brothers were hypocritical in their attitude towards their own blood-guiltiness; and we see the same hypocrisy in the attitude of the Jews towards the death penalty which they demanded against Jesus.

Sold — for the Price of a Slave

Let us come back to Joseph. Reuben was not present at all the discussions that took place, and he had the idea of returning to the pit and rescuing Joseph as soon as he could. While he was temporarily absent the other older brothers of Joseph sold him to a caravan of passing merchants. The brothers sold him as a slave, and their selling price of 20 pieces of silver was later recognized as the lowest price for which a useful slave could be sold. That is shown in the Bible in Leviticus 27:5.

Again we are reminded of the Lord Jesus Christ. Joseph was sold by his own brethren for 20 pieces of silver; and Jesus was sold by one of His chosen followers for 30 pieces of silver. At that time, as in the case of Joseph, that was the current price of a slave. In each historical action the background is correct.

Then the brothers took Joseph's splendid coat (a sign of special favor), and dipped it in the blood of a goat. They took this to their father Jacob, and told him they had found it. They asked whether or not it was Joseph's coat, and of course Jacob knew it was, and he was terribly distressed. Here Reuben must share the blame with his other brothers, for he, too, allowed his father to believe that Joseph had been killed by some wild animal.

Joseph took bread to his brothers and, as discussed earlier, he had "gone into death." In a sense he was a type of Jesus. Jesus, too, was sent to His brethren, sent by the loving Heavenly Father. We read in John 1:11, "He came to His own, and His own did not receive Him," and in John's Gospel we find that He is the sent one, sent by the Father to be the bread of God to those who will receive Him. He did not only bring bread, for He himself was the bread of God, sent from the very presence of the Father (John 6:33, 41, 51, 58).

In the picture of Jacob sorrowing we have one of those rare illustrations of the sorrow of our loving Heavenly Father when His Son was rejected and then crucified. For the gospel story is not only that the Son of God loved us: the triune godhead loved us, and we read that God was in Christ reconciling the world to himself. In the record of Abraham and Isaac we read that they, the father and the son, went both of them, together, to the place of sacrifice, and in John 3:16 we read that God so loved the world that He gave His only begotten Son. He gave Him up to die so that we could be redeemed by His precious blood. Is it any wonder that the writer of the epistle to the Hebrews asked, "How shall we escape if we neglect so great a salvation?" For when we face the issues of Calvary we must take sides. Either we are in a worse position than those guilty brothers of Joseph, or we are on the side of Jesus Christ. Either we have accepted Him as Saviour or we have not.

The brothers sold Joseph into slavery because they would not have him to reign over them. Just as surely today there are those who cry, "Away with Him, crucify Him! We will not have this man reign over us!" Others say with the apostle Peter, "You are the Christ. You are the Son of the living God" (Matt. 16:16). With Thomas they worship, exclaiming, "My Lord and my God!"

A greater-than-Joseph is here!

From Prison to Palace

Time and space do not allow us to consider the story of Joseph in detail. Joseph was unjustly put into prison, being found guilty of an offence he did not commit, but even in prison he acted as the servant of God and was put in charge of the other prisoners. Eventually he correctly interpreted the dreams of the pharaoh and was promoted from prison to palace. By his wisdom and able statesmanship, the most serious effects of famine were dealt with, and Joseph himself was second only to the pharaoh in power. He was given three titles, and these are referred to in Genesis 45:8 — "father to pharaoh," "lord of all his house," and "ruler of all Egypt" — this last title meant the two lands (of North and South Egypt). Spiritual lessons from these titles are elaborated in our section "Joseph in Egypt."

Paul the Apostle wrote to the Philippians and told them that in a coming day "every knee shall bow" to Christ. In Egypt the people had to bow as Joseph's royal chariot passed by. This was not just true of the loyal band of the palace owning him as "lord of the house." All Egyptian subjects bowed the knee, recognizing Joseph as next to the pharaoh. The day is coming when the Son of God will receive His kingdom, and "every knee shall bow." We who are Christians reverently and lovingly bow the knee now, in worship, as we call him Lord. But in a coming day even those outside the "house," His Church, will have to acknowledge His sceptre. He shall rule over all. A greater-than-Joseph is here.

Joseph was given the daughter of a priest as his wife. By Hebrew standards she was a Gentile, and in this there is a parallel with our heavenly Joseph. Jesus Christ is not just the chief minister of the land of Egypt, for He is King of kings and Lord of lords. Yet He left His royal palace to be born in a cattle stall. He came to die, and He, like Joseph, was to be given a Gentile bride, for one of the names of the Church is the bride of Christ. In that Church, Jew and Gentile become one in Christ.

Joseph did not provide only for the Egyptians, but for his own family also, and the story of his forgiveness of his brothers is well-known. Eventually they came to Egypt and showed the sincerity of their repentance for their earlier wickedness, and Joseph frankly forgave them and provided a wonderful feast for them. It was then that he used the three titles referred to above. He also saw to it that good provision was made for his aged father Jacob and the rest of the clan. They settled in the land of Goshen, a fertile part of Egypt.

Parallels with Our Heavenly Joseph: a Summary

We pause to consider briefly, and to summarize some of the remarkable ways in which Joseph prefigured the Lord Jesus Christ. Joseph was a shepherd in his early occupation, and Jesus described himself as the "Good Shepherd." Joseph was especially loved of his father, and our Lord was especially loved of His Heavenly Father who declared from heaven, "This is My beloved Son in Whom I am well pleased" (Matt. 3:17; 17:5).

Joseph was sent to his brethren, but he was rejected by those brothers, and they conspired against him. Jesus also was sent by His Father. He came to His own, and His own did not receive Him (John 1:11). They took deliberate counsel to slay Him, and, just as Joseph was stripped, so also was the Lord Jesus Christ stripped at the mockery of His trial. Joseph was hated because of his words to his brothers, and the Lord Jesus Christ was rejected when He presented teaching in words so convincing that even those sent to arrest Him declared, "No man ever spoke like this Man!" (John 7:46).

Though Joseph was rejected by his brothers, and they resented his dreams, yet those dreams came to fulfilment. Joseph DID rule over his brothers, just as his dreams foretold . . . and although Jesus' own people, the Jews, resented His claims, He, too, will reign over those who rejected Him. During His public ministry His claims to messiahship were bitterly opposed. Even on the cross He was taunted and mocked, as He himself had foretold. He rose triumphantly from the tomb, able to tell His disciples, "All authority has been given to Me in heaven and on earth" (Matt. 28:18). The Jews had said, "We will not have this man to reign over us" but God has decreed that in a coming day every knee will bow and acknowledge His sovereignty. As the well-known hymn puts it:

Jesus SHALL reign where'er the sun, Doth its successive journeys run.

Joseph's brothers conspired to sell him for a few pieces of silver, and Jesus also was sold for silver after His own people conspired against Him. Joseph was imprisoned, and the day came when the Son of God, the Creator of the heavens and the earth, allowed HIMSELF to be bound, and then to be taken as a prisoner.

Two Prisoners . . . and Two Crucified Thieves

Joseph was in prison with two others, one of whom knew a release to joy and happiness, and the other met a dreadful fate, and Jesus also suffered with two malefactors, one of whom knew a release when he died, for Jesus had told him, "Today you will be with Me in paradise" (Luke 23:43). The other prisoner, who had not repented of his sin and had reviled the Lord Jesus Christ even as he himself was dying, knew only the darkness of death and judgment.

Joseph did not attempt to defend himself when he was falsely accused, and in the Bible we read that when Jesus was reviled, He reviled not again. When He stood before Pilate He did not say so much as one word in His own defense. What He did say could have helped Pilate inherit the salvation of his soul, but Jesus did not say anything to defend himself. Pilate's situation was different from that of Herod who should have known of the prophesied Messiah.

Joseph won the respect of the man who was in charge of him in prison, and when Jesus died we read that the Roman centurion in charge of the crucifixion cried, "Certainly this was a righteous man" (Luke 23:47).

Despite the opposition of his brethren and of others, at the right time Joseph was delivered from the prison, and he was exalted. God was over-ruling . . . and though the very nation to which Jesus belonged clamoured for Him to be put into prison, and then to be crucified, at the right time God raised Him from the dead. We read in Acts 2:32, "This Jesus God has raised up." Men were allowed to bind Him, and they were even allowed to crucify Him, but death could not hold Him. At the right moment of time the seals of the tomb were broken and Jesus came forth. He was victorious over death and over the forces of evil.

Joseph was given a Gentile bride who was to comfort him in his exile from his father's house, and Jesus has been given a bride, His Church, and that bride is today going forth to Him outside the camp, bearing His reproach (Heb. 13:13).

Toward the end of the story we find Joseph providing bread for his brethren when it was impossible for them to be provided for anywhere else. They had sold him, yet Joseph forgave them, and provided for them out of his abundance. Jesus was sold by His brethren, yet He cried on the cross, "Father, forgive them, for they do not know what they do" (Luke 23:34). Not only did He forgive them, but those who come to Him today find that they, too, are forgiven and provided for with spiritual food not available elsewhere. There is no other source of spiritual satisfaction: spiritually there is a famine apart from Him who is the bread of God sent down from heaven.

Our Lord offers spiritual food, satisfaction. He offers abundance instead of famine, and spiritual wealth instead of poverty, to all those who will come to Him in their need. Joseph had resources which were greater than his brothers would have dreamed of, and he provided abundantly for them, and Jesus Christ has unlimited resources for all those who come to Him. "Come to Me, ALL you who labour and are heavy laden," He says, "and I will give you rest" (Matt. 11:28). He has infinite capacity, and can meet each of us in our many and varied needs. Just as Joseph provided for his brothers in a strange land, so spiritually (and materially, also) the Lord Jesus Christ can and does provide for His followers during their pilgrim journey.

Glory after Suffering

The brothers of Joseph went back to their father to tell him all about the glory of Joseph in Egypt, and the follower of the Lord Jesus Christ also delights to speak of HIS glory. To the Christian the Lord Jesus Christ is the altogether lovely one, the chiefest of ten thousand. The Christian gladly acknowledges Him as the Lord of glory.

One last point. At the Exodus from Egypt Joseph's bones were carried out of Egypt into the Promised Land of Canaan. Before he died, Joseph left instructions that this should be done, and the promise then given was carried out by the sons of a later generation. Here is just a faint picture of the resurrection of Christ, but He was not dependent on the fulfilling of a promise by another. He said himself that He lay down His life that He might take it again. A greater-than-Joseph is here, even He who said, "I am the resurrection and the life" (John 11:25).

All this leads us to the thought expressed in our opening verse — "Every knee shall bow . . . Jesus Christ is Lord!" The brothers of Joseph did not think they would ever bow before him, but the prophecy was fulfilled. God's Word is sure. A greater-than-Joseph is now here. In God's time EVERY knee WILL bow in reverence before Him, and every tongue WILL confess that Jesus Christ is Lord, to the glory of God the Father (Phil. 2:9–11) .

Brief Answers to Some Commonly Asked Questions about the Early Chapters of Genesis

1. Question: When did creation take place?

Answer: A few thousand years ago. Exodus 20:11 clearly states that everything in heaven and earth was created in six days.

2. Question: Don't modern dating methods show that such a belief is unacceptable?

Answer: There are many pointers to the recency of creation. The best known method of radio-metric dating is the carbon-14 method, usable only for dating organic materials. Most living things absorb carbon-14 while they are living: they do not discharge it after death. The C-14 decomposes into nitrogen.

The great majority of listed radio-carbon dates are less than 15,000 years, though often millions of years were expected by "establishment" scientists. Conversely, sometimes living things have been dated as ancient — e.g. a living shell was carbon dated at 2,300 years, mortar from an English castle of A.D. 1200 was dated to 7,370 years, and a seal mummified for 30 years was given a date of 4,600 years. All carbon dates, especially beyond the biblical Flood, are challengeable. What dramatic atmospheric changes took place at the Flood? Also, "constants" consistently turn out to be "variables," after all.

It is recognized that radio-carbon has not yet reached equilibrium of about 30,000 years, pointing to a date of the earth's atmosphere of 10 to 13,000 years. Carbon dates of less than 50,000 years (not millions) have been given to some samples of coal, oil, and natural gas. There are examples of fossilized tree trunks extending through several layers of coal — thus, all layers were deposited *after* the tree was in position, probably deposited by the Flood.

The decay of the earth's magnetic field, the amount of helium in the atmosphere, the breakup of star clusters, the growth rate of stalagtites and stalagmites, all the present phenomena, point to a young earth, only thousands of years old.

3. Question: Were the days of Genesis literal 24-hour days?

Answer: Yes. Where a numeral is linked with *yom* (day), it means 24 hours. This is also true with the expression used in Genesis, "The evening and the morning." This is a clear pointer to actual days as we know them.

Not only does the Bible point to literal days, but so does "nature." Plants need insects, and insects need plants, yet they were created on separate days. The time between could not be of the order of millions of years or thousands of years or even just years. The Genesis record with six literal days is indicated.

4. Question: If the days were 24 hours in length, how is it that the sun was there only on the fourth day?

Answer: We are not ancient Egyptian sun-worshipers, expecting the sun to be there as the first (impersonal) power. God himself spoke, and light appeared on the first day. He knows how long 24 hours is, and on the fourth day He established the sun as the light-bearer to regulate the light He had already created.

Astronomy explains the day and the night because of the earth's daily rotation around the sun, the 28-day month because of the monthly rotation of the moon around the earth, and the year because of the earth's annual revolution around the sun.

A DAY DEPENDS ON ROTATION, NOT REVOLUTION. It is the biblical revelation that uniquely explains the origin of the seven-day week.

This is not just a spiritual explanation — the model given in Genesis has a habit of fitting the facts. Sometimes the Bible revelation is ahead of the uncertainties of science. That fact of revelation means its statements are not limited by man's scientific knowledge.

5. Question: Some Bible believers argue that Genesis 1:2 should be translated, "And the earth became without form and void." Why do many scholars reject that translation?

Answer: They consider that theological implications rule it out, for this translation implies an activity that rendered God's original creation plan imperfect. They reject the idea of Satan's fall involving activity that caused the earth to become a dark, formless mass.

Rather, they see Genesis 1:1 as a preliminary statement surveying the whole picture which is then elaborated in greater detail.

6. Question: Do you reject the "gap theory" on theological grounds?

Answer: Yes. The word "was" is simply part of the common verb "to be." It occasionally has the meaning of "became," but to build a doctrine on one possible translation of a word seems to be a wrong approach to sound biblical exegesis. The doctrine that develops from this translation has great relevance to sin, judgment, and redemption, and it is reasonable to believe that the teaching would have been made clearer in other parts of Scripture if it was according to truth.

Teachings of the Bible do not need to depend on isolated words. Important truths are developed in various parts of Scripture, but no clear case is established for the "gap theory" by appealing to a possible translation of one word in a way that seems to be out of proportion to the consequent teaching.

Another point should be made. When the "gap theory" was first espoused, it seemed to be established that the world was at least millions of years old, largely because of the fossil evidence. Now it is known that almost all fossils can be explained by the flood of Noah's time, and long ages were not involved in their formation. The "gap theory" held firmly by many sincere Christians is both unnecessary and non-factual.

7. Question: What do you think Isaiah was referring to when he said concerning the earth, "He created it not in vain" (Isa. 45:18)?

Answer: Those who hold to the "gap theory" believe that this implies that the earth was not originally waste and void — that God did not create it "in vain." However, Isaiah was saying that when God created the heavens and earth there was a purpose. God is not limited in time as we are, and when we read the story of creation in Genesis 1 and 2 it is obvious that the crown of creation is man himself — the last recorded activity for the sixth day.

The earth was created for man to live upon, and the time that elapsed before man occupied it is in a sense virtually irrelevant in the great plan of the Eternal God. God's plan was that ultimately man would be placed on the earth, and so, as Isaiah says, "He created it not in vain."

But let's go on — the verse should be considered in full rather than selecting just part of it. It actually states, "He created it not in vain but for the habitation of man."

There is a very clear statement: There was a major purpose behind the creation of the earth — it was to be man's special home. And only the earth has the right atmospheric and other conditions to make it possible for life as we know it to exist. For example, it is just the right distance from the sun to avoid unbearable heat and unendurable cold. It is indeed created "for the habitation of man."

8. Question: Are science and the Christian religion regarded as mutually exclusive?

Answer: Certainly not. It is believed by many Christians that the God of the Bible and the God of nature are the same and so harmony, not mutual exclusion, should be our goal. A so-called Christian approach that automatically writes off the conclusions of "science" seems to me to be similar in spirit to a "scientific" approach that links all "Christian" belief with medieval superstition or brands it as uninformed and unenlightened obscurantism.

9. Question: When there is an apparent contradiction between science and the teachings of the Bible, which should be accepted?

Answer: Very many Christians believe that the Bible is the inspired and authoritative Word of God, and it is a court of final appeal. However, the word "apparent" is used in this question, and that allows an important qualification. When the seeming problems are looked at dispassionately over a period of time, it is often found that the difference is only "apparent" and not real after all.

10. Question: Does this mean that science always come to the biblical point of view, or vice versa?

Answer: Sometimes scientific theories are modified, and on the other hand sometimes it is necessary to have another look at what the Bible is really saying. The very fact that conservative Christians have been able to adapt themselves to different interpretations of Bible truth needs re-examination. I myself have become much more "literal" in my approach over the years. The evidence has convinced me of my need to change.

11. Question: Why should there be need for adapting oneself in that way — does not this suggest that we are changing Bible truth to fit so-called scientific knowledge?

Answer: There are areas where God has not given us all knowledge, and knowledge is often progressive. This is true in various fields. It does not take much thought to realize that there are many areas where there has been room for differing points of view, and for changing attitudes as knowledge has advanced. There is no need whatever for changing the Word of God itself. From time to time ancient words might become clearer because of new light from archaeology, or other fields of knowledge, but the original Word of God itself needs no changing. If God gives us further knowledge in the light of scientific advance, there is no reason why we should not study it to see if this fits somewhere into the revelation already given.

12. Question: Has science ever been right and the Bible wrong?

Answer: If by that you are referring to *interpretations* of Bible truth, yes, there have been times when science has been right.

When science first opposed the belief in a flat earth, again when it propounded the theory that the earth was not the center of all the heavenly creation, it was opposed most vigorously by orthodox churchmen. Today these teachings are seen as being in conformity to the teachings of the Bible, and they no longer cause concern.

13. Question: How do you relate science and the Bible?

Answer: The Bible is not widely recognized as a science textbook as such, though it touches on areas of science in an amazing way — such as when Peter wrote about a coming day when the elements would melt with fervent heat (2 Pet. 3:10, 12). The Bible uses language of phenomena, or appearance, and so can quite legitimately speak of the sun rising and setting.

This ancient book was originally written for an ancient people. And yet, implied within the very words of this record are facts which even today, with all our precision and scientific accuracy, are capable of interpretation which is acceptable to intelligent men.

Although the Bible is not a scientific textbook, it has never been shown to be in error at any point on which scientific knowledge is properly established.

I see science as examining the facts associated with the universe that God created, and in the Bible I find that these things are divinely ordained and continue to function to a divine plan.

The Bible can tell the scientist much about creation and the Creator, for what other acceptable revelation is there?

14. Question: Do you not agree that some scientists are opposed to the idea of revelation and the supernatural?

Answer: Of course — and so do many from other walks of life. However, when the scientist, as such, argues against revelation or the possibility of the supernatural, he has gone outside his field of specialized knowledge.

The fact that landing on the moon is outside my personal experience does not mean that this is such an incredible concept that it must be rejected out of hand.

15. Question: You do not think that the Genesis record is the story of man's searching after God, giving us a progressive understanding of God?

Answer: The first 11 chapters of the Bible have been called "the seed plot of the Bible" because in them we have the beginnings of essential doctrines. These are later elaborated and, in a sense, developed, but as soon as we come to particular doctrines in the Genesis record there is a consistent picture. That picture may be added to at later times, but it is never altered so far as the basic doctrines themselves are concerned.

16. Question: Then you reject the idea of an evolution of religion? You do not believe that we grope toward God until eventually we find Him in the New Testament revelation of Jesus Christ?

Answer: It is indeed true that the ultimate of the revelation of God is in the Person of Jesus Christ, for as the apostle Paul wrote, "In Him dwells all the fullness of the Godhead bodily" (Col. 2:9). However, it is also true that the picture of God in what we have called "the seed plot of the Bible" in Genesis 1 through 11 is a consistent picture. We learn there of the awful nature of sin, of the fallen nature of man, of the personality of the devil, and of the exalted nature of God.

He is the great Creator, the friend of man, the revealer, the grieving Father, the judge, the Redeemer, the restorer, the covenant keeper, the sustainer — there are marvelous seeds of doctrine in "the seed plot of the Bible."

In these chapters we learn of God's desire to walk with a man who will choose His way of holiness — and so we learn of God's interest in all men. It is little wonder that so many Bible students take these early chapters of Genesis so seriously!

17. Question: Can a Christian believe in theistic (God-controlled) evolution?

Answer: Many Christians do so believe, but they are wrong! The Bible declares that God rested after His creative acts — true creation ended at the end of the six days of creation — though changes within species do occur. The Bible knows nothing of "theistic evolution." As Professor E.H. Andrews puts it in *God, Science & Evolution:*

> We see, then, that by the tests of internal structure, context, and biblical testimony, the Genesis accounts of creation and the flood must be taken as entirely historical in intent. Those theistic evolutionists who teach otherwise do so on criteria that are wholly extra-biblical. . . . If Genesis is history, then regardless of the particular paradigm employed to record the historical events, the biblical testimony on creation and historical geology must be taken into account (and, indeed, conceded the primary place) in the construction of our cosmogenetical world view.[30]

The general argument of "theistic evolution" is that life has been God-given, and then has developed according to the general pattern of what is known as "evolution," but that God has controlled that evolution. One form of life has moved into the next, not by blind chance as a mere "survival of the fittest," but God has seen to it that the pattern is controlled along the lines which He himself allows.

On this argument, evolution is simply the means or method by which God has created. Genesis 1 is thus seen as a statement of the fact of creation, and God-controlled ("theistic") evolution is put forward as the method.

However, Hebrews 11:2 makes it clear that the worlds were not created from anything now visible. As we relate this to Genesis 1 we learn that man also was created at the express Word of God.

Creation is solely the act of God. He spoke and it was done — the acts of creation are the declaratory actions of God. Faith sees no problem in accepting the simple but majestic statements: "In the beginning God created . . ." and "So God created man in His own image."

18. Question: If one is not committed to a theory of theistic evolution, is there a particular view that can be shared?

Sometimes one hears the expression: "God's blueprint." We have seen that although man is a distinctive creation, this does not mean there is no similarity to other forms of creation.

On the contrary, such similarity is to be expected, for why should God throw away His "blueprint"? It is said of all creation that it was "very good," and so the life principle, the use of legs, the principles associated with the digestion of food — these and many other aspects can be pointed to, demonstrating that God did not "throw away the blueprint" when it had been used once.

In the knowledge of God, that "blueprint" was always there, not immediately fully or only revealed in a particular form of life, but completely known to Him. Thus, sometimes He used highly complex organs in a way that, according to an evolutionary theory, should not have been employed until much later in time.

A specific example of that is where the lowly trilobite turns up with about 500 other different forms of life in the so-called Cambrian strata, supposedly very early so far as fossils are concerned. The trilobite has both a simple and a compound eye. A compound eye is more complex than a modern camera lens, and its presence in the lowly trilobite cannot be satisfactorily explained by an evolutionary theory.

However, if we accept the concept of the all-powerful and all-knowing God who selected from His own "blueprint" according to His own wisdom, there is no problem. Also in God's "blueprint" was the spiritual being, man, known to God from before the foundation of the world (Eph. 1:4).

This highlights the uniqueness of man, for not only are there similarities because it is the one God who created all, but there are also qualities and characteristics in that "blueprint" which are reserved for man alone, the crown of God's creation.

So theistic evolution and creation are in fact incompatible. Theistic change and creation are reconcilable, but "evolution" has now come to include the concept of prime cause, and not just a secondary causation, nor a descriptive process of divine activity.

We believe in and accept changes of life forms within limits imposed by the Almighty Creator, but we also believe in special acts of creation — when "God spoke, and it was done."

Many who hold to theistic evolution argue that there were pre-Adamic creatures, with Adam "selected" from one of these. Romans 5 makes it clear that there was only one Adam. The doctrine of the Fall does not point to the evolution of man, but just the opposite. There was one original pair, Adam and Eve, directly the work of God in the sixth day of creation.

19. Question: Are there two gods — Elohim and Jehovah — in the Book of Genesis?

Answer: That was a major point in the Documentary Hypothesis that has been thoroughly discredited by archaeological findings. "Elohim" is the general name for God, in the masculine plural form — in fact, it is the "plural of majesty" (or "excellence") and points to more than two. "Jehoval" is believed to derive from the Hebrew verb "ro be," denoting existence: God is the ever-living One. As "Jehovah" (Yahweh) He enters into covenant relationship with His chosen people Israel.

In any case, other "gods" of ancient people were known by more than two names and the basic argument of the Documentary Hypothesis is shown to be without foundation.

Likewise, the hypothesis that there were different literary strands has been exposed as fallacious by continuing archaeological finds.

20. Question: Is it accepted that there have been changes in forms of life over the centuries?

Answer: Yes, of course — the evidence for that is very clear. To reject it would also mean denying changes by cross-fertilization of plants and animals in modern times. There we see the same sort of change, and though often these are man-controlled, it is by no means always the case. Changes have occurred in the animal and plant kingdoms in both ancient and modern times.

Actually, evolutionists must accept a fantastic theory of design if they follow their arguments to a logical conclusion: If we accept that all living things have descended from one single living cell, the inherent complexity of that one cell was miraculous indeed. Who designed its "components"? Who implanted the fantastic number of items of data inherent in just one cell — interdependent and inter-related?

21. Question: By agreeing to the fact of "change" is there not agreement to some form of evolution — what some might call "theistic evolution"?

Answer: No. The "agreeing" is to the possibility of change — to change of which the possibility is inherent within the relevant life forms themselves. It seems that evolution involves the taking on of completely new forms independently of the physiological and other limitations of the earlier form of life.

It can be accepted that changes of the type referred to are possible. Genesis 1:12 refers to trees yielding fruit whose seed was in itself, and so long as it is recognized that the derived life does come from its predecessors or precursors, there seems to be no reason at all why there should not be widely ranging variations of life forms as different "parents" are brought together.

22. Questions: Do not theistic evolutionists accept just that? If so, where are the points of difference?

Answer: There are many points at which the believer in theistic evolution and the man who believes in special creation come together. Many theistic evolutionists simply see evolution as God's *method* of creation, claiming that this is outside the scope of Genesis. However, all evolutionists must intimately recognize great leaps — gaps, if you like. At these points most theistic evolutionists would recognize the special creative activity of God. The fact is, many evolutionists will argue for "micro-evolution," with minimal changes within species. Many recognize that "macro-evolution" cannot be demonstrated. The lack of transitional forms in the fossil record has been a real headache to those arguing for evolution from only one primary blob of life, with chance rather than God in control.

23. Question: Can a person believe in evolution and at the same time be a Christian?

Answer: Before that question is answered, it should be clearly understood that salvation — truly being a Christian — does not depend on knowledge or on feelings, but on the great fact of personal belief in the Lord Jesus Christ who died because of our sins.

Many who have had a true experience of saving faith in Christ hold various wrong doctrines, but this does not mean that they are not "Christians." Many do not accept theistic evolution, for reasons made clear in this outline. However, many fine evangelical Christians do indeed believe in theistic evolution and, as already seen, they argue that this is God's method of creation.

24. Question: From where did Cain get his wife?

Answer: Genesis 5:4 makes it clear that Adam and Eve had other sons and daughters besides Cain and Abel. Cain would have had as his wife one of his sisters, or one of his nieces.

Mutational defects were not a problem in those early times. Indeed, Abraham married his half-sister Sarah. It was not until the time of Moses that such unions were forbidden. By then the original purity of the race had gone, and inter-family marriage was potentially dangerous to physical and mental health.

25. Question: Are we expected to believe that men such as Methuselah really lived to over 900 years?

Answer: The Sumerian King List, found at Kish, tells of a series of kings who lived between 10,800 and 64,800 years, "BEFORE THE FLOOD." The figures have clearly become exaggerated, but it is probably the fault of modern translators. It is now believed that the figures are not based on a decimal system, but on one with six as a base. This gives a total figure very close to the biblical total, but with differences in the individual lengths of life.

It seems that longevity and giantism were the order of the day before the Flood. Apparently, dramatic atmospheric and other changes took place when the vapor canopy around the earth was erupted.

Dinosaurs and huge mammoths appear to have died out as a result, and the Sumerian King List has men living for more "normal" periods of time soon after the Flood. A record from the city of Lagash also tells of astonishingly long life spans. Such traditions are also known in Egyptian, Chinese, and Roman records.

26. Question: Could the years have actually been months?

Answer: No. The ages given at which men could become fathers do not make sense if divided by 12 (for example, see Gen. 5:12, 15, 21). The fact that something is not happening today does not rule out its possible happening in previous times, especially if there is a dramatic explanation (Noah's flood) for changed conditions.

27. Question: What about the genealogical lists themselves — should they be taken literally?

Answer: Professor James Barr of the Oriental Institute at Oxford University in England wrote in a personal letter to David C. Watson on April 23, 1984: "Probably, so far as I know, there is no professor of Hebrew or Old Testament at any world-class university who does not believe that the writer(s) of Genesis 1—11 intended to convey to their readers the ideas that —

"(a) creation took place in a series of six days which were the same as the days of 24 hours we now experience.

"(b) the figures contained in the Genesis genealogies provided by simple addition a chronology from the beginning of the world up to later stages in the biblical story.

"(c) Noah's flood was understood to be worldwide and extinguish all human and animal life except for those in the ark.

"Or, to put it negatively, the apologetic arguments which suppose the 'days' of creation to be long eras of time, the figures of years not be chronological, and the flood to be a merely local Mesopotamian flood, are not taken seriously by any such professors, as far as I know. The only thing I would say to qualify this is that most such professors may avoid much involvement in that sort of argument and so may not say much explicitly about it one way or the other. But I think what I say would represent their position correctly."

28. Question: Did other peoples have similar records of their early history?

Answer: Only the Bible gives an acceptable history of a people for its actual development through individuals. Most other peoples start their written histories only when they are well established, when powerful kings are ruling, by which time the nation's early beginnings have been lost in antiquity. By comparison, the Hebrew people have a remarkable outline of their origins in Genesis 1 through 11.

29. Question: Is not Genesis merely a poetic record, not to be taken as actual fact?

Answer: Poetry does not precede prose, but comes after a nation is established. There is no reason to change that order, except to avoid the difficulty of accepting the literal nature of the Genesis record.

30. Question: Do other people have ideas of creation associated with a garden?

Answer: Yes — from an archaeological point of view, records which have been recovered deal with creation and tell of man's beginnings in a garden, directly created by the gods.

It is usually conceded that when different races have a common idea that is strongly developed, there is a basis of truth or an historical incident at the source of that belief. Why should the exception be the story of man's creation in a garden as told in the Bible in the early chapters of Genesis? In the same connection it is worth mentioning that no historical records have been found as to people who claimed that their beginnings were by descent or ascent from lower forms of life.

Those stories that are preserved tell of such matters as gods creating heaven and earth, of man coming directly from the gods, of man being immediately intelligent and civilized, of disease not being present, of plentiful food in a garden, and animals at peace in that garden. Then man offends the gods and is expelled from the garden so that misery and sorrow follow. Despite the polytheism in some of these records they yet have so much similarity to the story in Genesis that it is reasonable to assume that the Bible story is far more factual than many scholars would concede.

31. Question: Can you give one example of such a poetic presentation outside the Bible?

Answer: S.H. Hooke quotes as follows from the Sumerian *Epic of Enmerkar:*[31] (NEED INFO)

The land Dilmun is a pure place, the land Dilmun is a clean place,

The land Dilmun is a clean place, the land Dilmun is a bright place.

In dilmun the raven uttered no cry,

The kite uttered not the cry of the kite,

The lion killed not, The wolf snatched not the lamb,

Unknown was the kid-killing dog,

Unknown was the grain-devouring boar. . . .

The sick-eyed says not "I am sick-headed,"

Its (Dilmun's) old woman says not "I am an old woman,"

Its old man says not "I am an old man,"

Unbathed is the maid, no sparkling water is poured in the city,

Who crosses the river (of death?) utters no. . . .

The wailing priests walk not about him,

The singer utters no wail,

By the side of the city he utters no lament.

Of course, much of this is seen in its ideal in the new Jerusalem. The lion lies down with the lamb. There is no more weeping, and all tears are wiped away. The blessings of Eden are restored, and much more besides. The ancient world grasped after such a golden age, but its perfection is seen in the pages of the Bible, God's revelation to man — His Word of truth.

32. Question: Have you a comment as to the basic physiological differences between "white" and "black" races?

Answer: The following comment by William C. Boyd, professor of immunochemistry at the Boston University School of Medicine, is relevant:

> We should not be surprised if identical genes crop up in all corners of the earth, or if the overall racial differences we detect prove to be small. We do not know the total number of gene differences which mark off a Negro of the Alur tribe in the Belgian Congo from a white native of Haderslev, Denmark. Glass has suggested that the number of gene differences even in such a case is probably small. Besides a few genes for skin colour, he thinks that there may be a dominant gene for kinky hair and a pair or two of genes for facial features. He considers it unlikely that there are more than six pairs of genes in which the white race differs characteristically from the black. This estimate errs somewhat on the small side, in the opinion of the present writer. Probably, however, it is of the right order of magnitude, and any outraged conviction that the difference between the two races must be much greater than this, which some persons might feel, is likely to be based on emotional, rather than rational, factors.

Professor Boyd makes it clear that there is not so much difference between the races after all. As the apostle Paul says, "God has made of one blood all nations of men to dwell on all the face of the earth" (Acts 17:26).

Professor Boyd goes on to say:

> An inherited difference becomes vital as marking off a race only when someone chooses to treat it as vital. . . . A Semitic nose or a black skin is no more significant . . . than a head of flaming red hair. [32]

Much has been written as to differences brought about by climate and hereditary factors and it seems likely that when combined these could well be a sufficient explanation. Why should not those relatively insignificant hereditary factors be traced to the sons of Noah? Interestingly enough, it is the dark races who have an additional genetic structure as a protection against the sun. The presence of melanin in human skin causes darkness. "Black" people have a little more than "whites." The difference in quantity is quite small — yet melanin is a major factor as to the color of a person's skin.

33. Question: Who wrote the Book of Genesis?

Answer: P.J. Wiseman in his *New Discoveries in Babylonia about Genesis* put forward the argument that the literary aids demonstrated in Genesis indicate "that the book was compiled at an early date, certainly not later than the age of Moses." He suggested that the repetition of words and phrases pointed to different clay tablets, the first words of the new tablet being a repetition of the last words of the previous record — what is technically called a "colophon." He argued that this can be seen as follows:

Gen. 1:1:   "God created the heavens and the earth" (compare with Gen. 2:4)

Gen. 2:4:   "When they were created" (compare with Gen. 5:2)

Gen. 6:10:   "Shem, Ham and Japheth" (compare with Gen. 10:1)

Gen 10:1:   "After the flood" (compare with Gen. 11:10)

Gen. 11:26:   "Abram, Nahor and Haran" (compare with 11:27)

Gen. 25:12:   "Abraham's son" (compare with 25:19)

Gen. 36:1:   "Who is Edom" (compare with Gen. 36:8)

Gen. 36:9:   "Father of the Edomites" [literally "Father Edom"]
               (compare with Gen. 36:43)[33]

Wiseman adds convincing evidence to show similar practices from the written records of the ancient East — these early Bible records follow the recognized pattern. In these early chapters of Genesis we have the generations of the heavens and the earth (Gen. 2:4); of the first man Adam (Gen. 5:1); the three sons of Noah before the flood (Gen. 10:1); their later descendants until the birth of Abraham (Gen. 11:26); and a more detailed record of Abraham's immediate family — his father Terah, his brothers, etc. (Gen. 11:27). All this is an introduction to Abraham himself who now occupies a central place in the record.

All of the Book of Genesis was composed from various early documents and records, and there are evidences therein of very ancient writings, such as those of chapters 14 and 23. Traditionally it is believed that these records were eventually compiled by Moses as the first book of the Pentateuch, the latter being the first five books of the Bible. All the events of Genesis took place before Moses himself was born.

The Lord Jesus put His seal on the authenticity of the first five books of the Bible. We stand with Him.

Endnotes

[1] Personal communication from Dr. Henry Morris to Dr. Clifford Wilson and included in Pacific International University Course OTB 501 Genesis (Chapter 2). This printing 1996.

[2] Paolo Matthiae, *Ebla — An Empire Rediscovered* (Garden City, NY: Doubleday, 1981).

[3] Duane Gish, *Evolution: The Fossils Still Say No!* (El Cajon, CA: Institute for Creation Research, 1995).

[4] *Nature*, 258:389, 1975.

[5] Dr. Malcolm Bowden, *Ape-Men — Fact or Fallacy* (Bromley, England: Sovereign Publications, 1977).

[6] W.F. Albright, *Yahweh and the Gods of Canaan: An Historical Analysis of Two Contrasting Faiths* (New York, NY: Doubleday, 1968).

[7] Andrew Snelling — Personal communication made available to Dr. Clifford Wilson for *Creation/Evolution — Facts or Fairy Tales* (Melbourne, Australia: Pacific Christian Ministries, 1994).

[8] Stephen Langdon in *Semitic Mythology*, Vol. V, 1931.

[9] Donald Wiseman, *Illustrations from Biblical Archaeology* (London: Tyndale Press, 1958).

[10] Wiseman, *Illustrations from Biblical Archaeology.*

[11] Donald Wiseman, *Clues to Creation in Genesis* (London: Marshall, Morgan and Scott, 1977).

[12] Albright, *Recent Discoveries in Bible Lands* (New York, NY: Funk and Wagnalls, 1995), p. 70 ff.

[13] Edward F. Blick, *Correlating the Bible and Science* (Oklahoma City, OK: SW Radio Bible Church, 1976). See also *A Scientific Analysis of Genesis* (Oklahoma City, OK: Hearthstone Publishing Ltd., 1991).

[14] Raphael Kazmann, Louisiana State University Geotimes, 4/13/78.

[15] Harold S. Slusher, *Clues Regarding the Age of the Universe, in the Battle for Creation* (El Cajon, CA: Institute for Creation Research, 1976), p. 259.

[16] Lyall Watson, "The Water People," *Science Digest*, Vol. 90, May 1992, p. 10-11.

[17] Clifford Wilson, *Monkeys Will Never Talk — or Will They?* (Victoria, Australia: PCM Christian Press, 1996).

[18] Duane Gish, "Ape-Men — Fact or Fallacy?" *The Battle for Creation* (Green Forest, AR: Master Books, 1976).

[19] G.A. Kerkut, *Implications of Evolution* (New York, NY: Pergamon, 1960), p. 150.

[20] W.F. Albright, *The Biblical Period from Abraham to Ezra* (New York, NY: Harper & Row Torch Books, 1963), p. 15.

[21] Donald Wiseman, *Illustrations from Biblical Archaeology* (London: Tyndale Press, 1958).

[22] Howard F. Vos, *Archaeology in Bible Lands* (Chicago, IL: Moody Press, 1977).

[23] John B. Pritchard, ed., *Ancient Near Eastern Texts Relating to the New Testament* (Princeton, NJ: Princeton University Press, 1950).

[24]Zev Zilnay, *Israel Guide*, Jerusalem Achiever, 1969.

[25]Walter J. Beasley, *The Amazing Story of Sodom* (Bombay: Gospel Literature Service, 1957).

[26]Pritchard, *Ancient Near Eastern Texts Relating to the New Testament.*

[27]John Ankerberg, John Weldon, and Walter C. Kaiser, Jr., *The Case for Jesus the Messiah* (Chattanooga, TN: The John Ankerberg Evangelistic Association, 1989).

[28]Pritchard, *Ancient Near Eastern Texts Relating to the New Testament.*

[29]Kenneth A. Kitchen, *Ancient Orient and the Old Testament* (Downers Grove, IL: Inter-Varsity Press, 1966), p. 90.

[30]E.H. Andrews, *God, Science & Evolution* (Sydney, Australia: Anzea Books, 1980), p. 72.

[31]S.H. Hooke, *Middle Eastern Mythology* (New York, NY: Penguin/Pelican Books, 1963), p. 114.

[32]William C. Boyd, *Genetics and the Races of Man* (Blackwells Scientific Publications, 1950), p. 200.

[33]P.J. Wiseman, *New Discoveries in Babylonia about Genesis* (London: Marshall Morgan and Scott, 1936/ 1958).

Selective Bibliography

This bibliography is not complete. Much that is within the complete work of *The Bible Comes Alive* results from a lifetime of personal research and investigation, often on actual sites where no written records were available.

Albright, William Foxwell. *The Bible Period from Abraham to Ezra.* New York, NY: Harper & Row Torch Books, 1963.

Ankerberg, John, John Weldon, and Walter D. Kaiser Jr. *The Case for Jesus the Messiah.* Chattanooga, TN: The John Ankerberg Evangelistic Association, 1989.

Beasley, Walter J. *The Amazing Story of Sodom.* Bombay: Gospel Literature Service, 1957.

Bowden, Michael. *Ape-Man — Fact or Fallacy.* Bromley, England: Sovereign Publications, 1977.

Boyd, Robert T. *A Pictorial Guide to Biblical Archaeology.* Eugene, OR: Harvest House Publishers, Inc., 1981.

Breasted, James H. *A Brief History of Ancient Times.* London: Ginn and Co., 1967.

Bruce, Francis F. *Israel and the Nations.* Exeter, England: Paternoster Press, 1963.

Campbell, Edward F., and David N. Freedman, eds. *The Biblical Archaeologist Reader No. 3.* Garden City, NY: Anchor Books, Doubleday, 1970.

Clack, Clem. *The Bible in Focus.* Blackburn South, Victoria, Australia: Donors, Inc., 1980.

Davis, John J., and John C. Whitcomb. *A History of Israel.* Grand Rapids, MI: Baker Book House, 1980.

Finegan, Jack. *Light from the Ancient Past.* Princeton, NJ: Princeton University Press, 1959.

Gish, Duane T. *Evolution: The Fossils Still Say No.* El Cajon, CA: Institute for Creation Research, 1995.

Goff, Mike R.O. *Fodor's 90 Israel.* New York, NY: Fodor's-Random House, 1989.

Harrison, R.K. *Introduction to the Old Testament.* Grand Rapids, MI: Wm.B. Eerdmans Pub. Co., 1975.

———. *Old Testament Times.* Grand Rapids, MI: Wm.B. Eerdmans Pub. Co., 1970.

Harvey, Jeff, and Charles Pallagy. *The Bible and Science.* Blackburn, Victoria, Australia: Acacia Press, 1985.

Kitchen, Kenneth A. *Ancient Orient and Old Testament.* Downers Grove, IL: Inter-Varsity Press, 1966.

———. *The Bible in Its World.* Downers Grove, IL: Inter-Varsity Press, 1978.

Kramer, Samuel N. "The Babel of Tongues — A Sumerian Version." *American Oriental Society Journal* (March 1968).

Lehman, Manfred R. "Abraham's Purchase of Machpelah and Hittite Law." Bulletin of the American Schools of Oriental Research, no. 129 (February 1953).

Matthiae, Paolo. *Ebla — An Empire Rediscovered.* Garden City, NY: Doubleday, 1981.

Morris, Henry M. *The Genesis Record.* Grand Rapids, MI: Baker Book House, 1976.

———. *Evolution in Turmoil.* ??? 1982

———. *The Biblical Basis for Modern Science.* Grand Rapids, MI: Baker Book House, 1990.

Morris, Henry M., and Gary E. Parker. *What Is Creation Science?* Green Forest, AR: Master Books, 1982.

Murphy-O'Connor, Jerome. *An Archaeological Guide of the Holy Land.* New York, NY: Oxford University Press, 1986.

Oxnard, Charles. *Nature* (258:389), 1975.

Pfeiffer, Charles F., ed. *The Biblical World: A Dictionary of Biblical Archaeology.* Grand Rapids, MI: Baker Book House, 1966.

Pritchard, John B., ed. *Ancient Near Eastern Texts Relating to the New Testament.* Princeton, NJ: Princeton University Press, 1950.

————. *The Ancient Near East in Pictures Relating to the Old Testament.* Princeton, NJ: Princeton University Press 1954.

Rendle-Short, John. *Man: Ape or Image.* Sunnybank, Queensland, Australia: Creation Science Publishing, 1981.

Unger, Merrill F. *Archaeology and the Old Testament.* Grand Rapids, MI: Zondervan, 1954.

Vos, Howard F. *Archaeology in Bible Lands.* Chicago, IL: Moody Press, 1977.

Whitcomb, John, and Henry Morris. *The Genesis Flood.* Grand Rapids, MI: Baker Book House, 1989.

Whitelaw, Robert L. *Evolution and the Bible in the Light of 15,000 Radio Carbon Dates.* Sterling, VA: Grace Abounding Ministries, 1986.

Wilder-Smith, A.E. *The Natural Sciences Know Nothing of Evolution.* Green Forest, AR: Master Books, 1982.

Wilson, Clifford A. *That Incredible Book the Bible.* Melbourne, Australia: Word of Truth Productions, 1973.

————. *Rocks, Relics, and Biblical Reliability.* Grand Rapids, MI: Zondervan, 1977.

————. *Highlights of Biblical Archaeology.* Melbourne, Australia: Pacific College of Graduate Studies, 1985.

————. *Creation or Evolution: Facts or Fairytales?* Melbourne, Australia: Pacific College of Graduate Studies, 1991.

Wiseman, Donald. *Illustrations from Biblical Archaeology.* London: Tyndale Press, 1958.

Wiseman, P.J. *Clues to Creation and Genesis.* Professor Donald J. Wiseman, ed. London: Marshall Morgan and Scott, 1977.

Wood, Leon J. *A Survey of Israel's History.* Revised by David O'Brien. Grand Rapids, MI: Zondervan, 1986.

Woolley, C. Leonard. *Ur of the Chaldees.* London: Penguin Books, 1954.

Wright, G. Ernest. *Biblical Archaeology.* Philadelphia, PA: Westminster Press, 1962.

Zilnay, Zev. *Israel Guide.* Jerusalem: Ahiever, 1969.

Dr. Clifford Wilson is the founding president of
PACIFIC INTERNATIONAL UNIVERSITY

Professional training by academic education including extension studies.

Majoring in:
Bible and Theology
Biblical Archaeology
Christian Counseling
Christian Education
Christian Evidences
Christian Philosophy
Church Ministry
Comparative Religions
Linguistics
Trans-cultural studies and Missiology

You don't have to leave home to receive thorough training in Bible, Christian skills, and ministry.

Course are available at:
Certificate level
Diplomas
Bachelor Degrees
Master Degrees
Doctoral Degrees

Write for catalog:
P.O. Box 1717
(2158 N. Ramsey Ave.)
Springfield, MO 65801
(417) 831-7515
Fax (417) 831-7673